CHATELAINE
food express
Starters

CHATELAINE food express

Starters

GREAT BEGINNINGS
FROM APPETIZERS TO SOUPS

BY MONDA ROSENBERG

M&S

A SMITH SHERMAN BOOK
produced in conjunction with CHATELAINE®
and published by McCLELLAND & STEWART INC.

CHATELAINE

Canadian Cataloguing in Publication Data

Rosenberg, Monda
    Starters: great beginnings from appetizers to soups

(Chatelaine food express)
"A Smith Sherman book produced in conjunction with Chatelaine"
Includes index
ISBN 0-7710-7594-4

1. Appetizers. I. Title.   II. Series.

TX740.R67 1999   641.8'12   C99-931695-8

ACKNOWLEDGEMENTS

Few in life are lucky enough to find a team of workmates with whom they feel privileged to be associated. I've been blessed in this regard both in my collaboration with Smith Sherman Books Inc. in producing the Food Express series of cookbooks and in my association with my colleagues at CHATELAINE magazine. I owe great appreciation to Carol Sherman and Andrew Smith, who massage and manipulate our recipes into such appealing and beautiful books. Thanks to Joseph Gisini and Jonathan Freeman, who fine-tune every tiny detail of the design, Bernice Eisenstein for her flawless copyediting, Erik Tanner for all his help and Margaret Swain for permission to use some of her beverage recipes. My sincere thanks also to the CHATELAINE Test Kitchen team, spearheaded by Marilyn Crowley and Trudy Patterson, who tested every recipe until they simply could not be improved upon; Deborah Aldcorn for her hawk-eyed editing; editor Rona Maynard for her constant caring and input; publisher Donna Clark, and Lee Simpson and Cheryl Smith for their strong commitment to this project; the CHATELAINE creative team of art director Caren Watkins and creative associate Barb Glaser; our world-class team of photographer Ed O'Neil, creative director Miriam Gee and food stylist Rosemarie Superville. Thanks to the entire McClelland & Stewart family, particularly editor Pat Kennedy for her constant support; and Alison Fryer and Jennifer Grange from the Cookbook Store for their sage advice.

MONDA ROSENBERG

COVER PHOTO: TOMATO-PRAWN BRUSCHETTA, *see recipe page 13*

PHOTO PAGE 2: CHICKEN & SHIITAKE SOUP WITH COCONUT MILK, *see recipe page 133*

CREDITS: *see page 143*   PRINTED AND BOUND IN CANADA

A CELEBRATION OF COCKTAILS, CANAPÉS AND OTHER GREAT BEGINNINGS

Impress from the very first bite with **Starters**. Whether you call them canapés, appetizers or hors d'oeuvres, they are the first seductive bites that set the stage for the rest of the evening. A tray of pretty appetizers, a bowl of spiced nuts, a refreshing drink or an easygoing soup or salad can provide a "wow" beginning for the rest of the meal.

You have better things to do than spend a long time fiddling with appetizers or first-course offerings. So here are recipes that can be whipped up whether you're throwing a fashionable cocktail party or you simply need a few nibbles to accompany drinks before dinner. There's even recipes for the drinks! Most of these recipes can be made ahead. A lot can be tucked into the freezer for instant reheating in the microwave or oven and some just need a little stirring and spreading before the doorbell rings.

In **Starters** you'll find a stunning antipasto, robust stilton shortbread nibblers, festive barbecued chicken wings and exotic island shrimp to mention a few. Beyond appetizers, there's colorful first courses from sublime soups and spicy salads to soothing risottos. All make first-class beginnings while leaving room for the big-time entrées. Most of our impressive first courses can be completely finished and some even plated before guests arrive.

Starters **will ease your opening concerns and let you sit back with your guests, relax and enjoy the raves.**

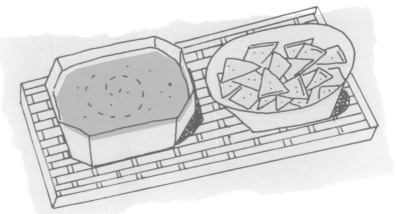

CONTENTS

APPETIZERS ◆ Cold

*Creamy chèvre spiked with hot pepper sauce
is a seductive base for roast beef furls in these
RED PEPPER CANAPÉS (see recipe page 10).*

APPETIZERS ◆ Cold

RED PEPPER CANAPÉS

This substantial party nibble is from Therese Taylor of Dan T's Inferno. Choose your own level of "fire."

Stir together
    4.5-oz (140-g) roll chèvre
      or 4-oz (125-g) pkg cream cheese
    2 to 4 tbsp hot pepper sauce such as Dan T's
      Spiced Cayenne Sauce
Pit and cut into chunks
    ⅓ cup black olives
In a saucepan, heat
    1 tbsp olive oil
Stir in
    2 thinly sliced seeded red peppers
    1 large minced garlic clove
Sauté until peppers are softened, about
    10 minutes. Meanwhile, slice crosswise
    into ¼-inch (0.5-cm) thick rounds
    1 long baguette
Lightly broil about 2 minutes per side. Spread
    with cheese mixture. Cover each slice with
    1 piece of arugula, 1 small bunch total
    1 furled thin slice of cooked roast beef,
      about ½ lb (250 g) total
Scatter with a few sautéed peppers.
Dot with several pieces of olive.
    Makes: 32 canapés

        PREPARATION: 15 MINUTES
          COOKING: 10 MINUTES
          BROILING: 4 MINUTES

MAKE AHEAD: Prepare cheese mixture, olive pieces and sautéed peppers. Cover separately and refrigerate for up to 2 days. Then continue with recipe.

BRIE WITH SUN-DRIED TOMATOES

These quick and easy nibbles are a classy alternative to chips and dip.

Soak in warm water for 45 minutes
    ¼ cup sun-dried tomatoes
    Or use sun-dried tomatoes in oil.
Drain, then whirl in a food processor until
    coarsely ground with
    2 garlic cloves
    2 tbsp chopped parsley
    pinch of ground black pepper
Spread over top of
    4-inch (10-cm) round cold Brie
      or Camembert
Bake on a baking sheet in a 350°F (180°C) oven,
    10 minutes, or microwave on medium, just
    until the sides feel warm, about 1½ minutes.
Serve at room temperature with crackers or
    sliced baguettes.
    Makes: 4 to 8 appetizers

        PREPARATION: 10 MINUTES
          BAKING: 10 MINUTES

MAKE AHEAD: Prepare Brie with tomato mixture and cover loosely with plastic wrap. Refrigerate for up to 2 days before heating.

POSH PICNIC SEAFOOD ROLLS

*Portable and perfect for informal dining, these appetizer rolls are great for
a sophisticated picnic or knockout barbecue.*

Stir together
- 1 lb (454 g) cooked small shrimp
- 8 oz (250 g) cooked crab
- 6.5-oz (184-g) can drained flaked salmon or tuna
- 1 cup grated carrot
- 1 finely diced celery stalk
- 2 minced seeded jalapeños
- 2 sliced green onions

In another bowl, stir together
- ¾ cup light mayonnaise
- ⅓ cup chopped fresh dill
- finely grated peel of 1 lime
- ¼ tsp white pepper

Mix with seafood. Slice in half lengthwise
- 2 (24-inch/60-cm) French baguettes

Hollow out centres, leaving a shell about 1 inch (2.5 cm) thick. Mound seafood filling in bottom. Sprinkle with
- 2 cups shredded lettuce

Replace tops. Wrap in plastic wrap and refrigerate up to half a day. Slice into serving-size pieces.

Makes: 10 appetizers

PREPARATION: 30 MINUTES

POSH PICNIC SEAFOOD ROLLS

APPETIZERS ◆ Cold

EASY ANTIPASTO

Store-bought antipasto is pricey. This homemade version is sensibly priced and terrific.

In a large bowl, whisk together
⅔ cup olive oil
¼ cup freshly squeezed lemon juice
3 minced garlic cloves
1 tsp dried basil
¼ tsp freshly ground black pepper
Arrange on a large platter with shallow sides
¾ lb (375 g) thickly sliced mushrooms
14-oz (398-g) can drained artichoke
hearts, halved
1 sliced small red onion
1 sliced English cucumber
1 julienned zucchini
Drizzle dressing over top. Cover and marinate
2 hours at room temperature or overnight in
refrigerator. Just before serving, add to platter
2 (6.5-oz/184-g) cans drained tuna
or 2 cups cooked small shrimp
3 hard-boiled eggs, cut into wedges
16 tiny cherry tomatoes
Serve antipasto platter surrounded with
baguette slices.
Makes: 8 to 10 servings

PREPARATION: 20 MINUTES
MARINATING: 2 HOURS

CAVIAR ARTICHOKE HEARTS

Appetizers don't have to take hours to prepare. These quick nibblers take just minutes to make.

Drain and pat dry
14-oz (398-mL) can artichoke hearts
Spoon into each centre
1 tsp sour cream
Top with
½ tsp red or black caviar or a little of both
Serve right away.
Makes: 6 to 8 hearts

PREPARATION: 5 MINUTES

SMOKED OYSTER ROLLS

These rolls are an easy and sophisticated version of party sandwiches.

Drain
3-oz (85-g) can smoked oysters
Pat dry and finely chop. Stir in
8-oz (250-g) pkg spreadable cream cheese
2 finely sliced green onions
dash of Worcestershire
Trim crusts from
12 slices white bread
Spread about 2 tbsp filling over each slice. Roll
up tightly. Wrap in plastic wrap and twist
ends. Refrigerate for at least 30 minutes or
overnight. Slice roll into rounds.
Makes: 72 pieces

PREPARATION: 10 MINUTES
REFRIGERATION: 30 MINUTES

TOMATO-PRAWN BRUSCHETTA

This superb recipe by chef Lesley Stowe is from the cookbook
The Girls Who Dish: Top Women Chefs Cook Their Best *(Whitecap, 1998).*

Coarsely chop
    1 lb (500 g) cooked prawns or shrimp
    (See Shrimp Savvy, page 15, for buying and
    cooking shrimp.)
Place in a large bowl. Stir in
    grated peel of 1 lemon
    1 tsp freshly squeezed lemon juice
    2 tbsp capers
    3 tbsp chopped fresh basil
    4 minced garlic cloves
    ¼ cup olive oil

Then stir in
    1 ½ cups diced seeded plum tomatoes
    1 diced peeled avocado (optional)
Season with
    salt and pepper
Heap on
    toasted baguette slices
Also wonderful on salad greens. Refrigerated,
    mixture will keep well for half a day.
    Makes: 4 cups

PREPARATION: 15 MINUTES
TOASTING: 2 MINUTES

TOMATO-PRAWN BRUSCHETTA

APPETIZERS ◆ Cold

CURRIED TUNA MINI PITAS

These tiny perfect stuffed pitas are great for summer nibbling or poolside noshing.

Stir together
   6.5-oz (184-g) can drained flaked tuna
   2 tbsp mayonnaise
   2 tsp freshly squeezed lemon juice
   ½ tsp curry powder
Stir in
   1 finely chopped small red-skinned apple
Cut in half
   10 mini pitas
Spoon tuna mixture into each. Then top with
   a few alfalfa sprouts
Makes: 20 mini pitas

PREPARATION: 5 MINUTES

MAKE AHEAD: Fill pitas with tuna mixture. Refrigerate in a sealed container for up to a day. Add sprouts just before serving.

SHRIMP WITH CHEATER AIOLI

Serve guests a pile of shrimp to peel and dip into this fast garlicky mayonnaise.

Stir together
   1 cup light mayonnaise
   2 to 3 large minced garlic cloves
   2 tbsp finely chopped fresh parsley
     or coriander
   ¼ tsp cayenne or black pepper
Cook
   3 lbs (1.5 kg) fresh or frozen uncooked
     large shrimp
in boiling water until shrimp turn pink, from 3 to 4 minutes. Immediately drain shrimp and serve.
Makes: 8 to 10 servings

PREPARATION: 10 MINUTES
COOKING: 4 MINUTES

MAKE AHEAD: Cover and refrigerate mayonnaise mixture for up to 2 days. Cook shrimp, spread out on metal tray and refrigerate immediately. When cold, place in a bag and seal for up to a day. Serve shrimp cold.

Curried Tuna Mini Pitas

Smoked Salmon & Spinach Swirls

Oh-so-easy to make, these party rolls are very elegant with swirls of pink and green.
Just a few minutes of spreading and rolling yield appetizers for a big party.

Spread
   6 tortillas, about 7 inches (18 cm) wide
   with
   8-oz (250-g) pkg spreadable cream cheese
Sprinkle with
   2 thinly sliced green onions
   1 tbsp chopped drained capers
   grindings of black pepper
Add a single layer of
   spinach leaves with stems removed,
      about 10-oz (284-g) bag

Don't completely cover cheese. Scatter with
   3 oz (120 g) thinly sliced smoked salmon
      or smoked salmon bits
Press down slightly, then tightly roll up tortillas.
   Wrap in plastic wrap and refrigerate at least
   2 hours or overnight.
Serve sliced in 1-inch (2.5-cm) rounds.
   Makes: 48 pieces

PREPARATION: 15 MINUTES
REFRIGERATION: 2 HOURS

Tips

Snazzy Deviled Eggs
Jazz up deviled eggs with these tips. Mash about
¼ cup mayonnaise and pinches of salt and pepper
with 6 egg yolks:

- Add a finely chopped dill pickle or 2 tbsp
  chopped fresh dill.

- Replace half the mayonnaise with sour cream.
  Add a little grated onion and chopped capers.
  Top with slices of smoked salmon.

- Add crumbled cooked bacon, a dab of Dijon
  and sliced green onions or chives.

- Replace 1 tbsp mayonnaise with 1 tbsp mango
  chutney and add a generous sprinkle of curry
  powder.

- Add pinches of cayenne pepper or chopped
  canned hot pepper.

Shrimp Savvy
Whatever the size, here are some tips for ensuring
firm, sweet-tasting shrimp:

- Shrimp should be sweet smelling with no whiff
  of iodine. Keep refrigerated or frozen until ready
  to use because they spoil quickly.

- Defrost frozen cooked shrimp in a sieve
  under cold running water, then pat dry with
  paper towels.

- Cook raw shrimp just until pink following
  minimum package or recipe time.

APPETIZERS ◆ Hot

*Beautiful biriyani-tossed shrimp are teamed
with a seductive sauce for dipping in this
SHRIMP WITH MANGO-LIME SAUCE
(see recipe page 18).*

SHRIMP WITH MANGO-LIME SAUCE

This sensational appetizer is from Colleen Walker, a co-owner of Catered Affare in Toronto.

Remove shells, leaving tail attached, on
    1 lb (500 g) fresh or frozen uncooked
      large shrimp
In a large bowl, stir together
    ¼ cup olive oil
    2 tbsp freshly squeezed lime juice
    2 tbsp biriyani or curry paste or 1 tbsp each
      curry powder and ground cumin
    ¼ tsp cayenne
Add shrimp and toss until coated. Cover and
    refrigerate from 2 to 4 hours or overnight.
For sauce, in a food processor, purée
    1 pitted peeled large ripe mango
    finely grated peel of 1 lime
    1 tbsp sherry
Add and whirl until coarsely chopped
    ¼ cup lightly packed fresh coriander leaves
Drain shrimp and spread out on a foil-lined
    baking sheet. Roast at 375°F (190°C)
    until pink, about 5 minutes. Grasp by
    tail for dipping into mango sauce or
    serve on skewers.
Makes: 6 appetizer servings and about
1½ cups sauce

PREPARATION: 20 MINUTES
MARINATING: 2 HOURS
BAKING: 5 MINUTES

MAKE AHEAD: Shrimp can be marinated a day ahead. Shrimp can be baked, then refrigerated and served cold. Sauce keeps in refrigerator for at least a day.

NOTE: Biriyani and curry paste is sold in Indian stores and condiment sections of supermarkets.

CURRIED PARTY SHRIMP

Make this dish the centrepiece of your party. Serve in a chafing dish and let guests help themselves.

For sauce, stir together
    3 large chopped seeded tomatoes
      or 2 cups drained canned diced tomatoes
    ¾ cup unsweetened coconut milk
      or ¼ cup whipping or table cream
    2 tsp grated fresh ginger or ½ tsp bottled
      minced ginger
    1½ tsp each ground cumin and ground
      coriander
    ½ tsp each turmeric and salt
    ¼ tsp cayenne or 2 tbsp minced jalapeños
Remove shells, leaving tail attached, on
    1 lb (500 g) fresh or frozen uncooked
      medium-size shrimp
In a lightly oiled large nonstick frying pan
    over medium-high, heat
    1 tbsp yellow or black mustard seeds
    shaking pan often until popping.
Stir in
    3 minced garlic cloves or 1½ tsp bottled
      minced garlic
Add shrimp and
    juice of ½ lemon
Add sauce. Stir shrimp often until sauce starts
    to bubble. Reduce heat to low and continue
    simmering, stirring often, about 5 minutes.
    Spoon a little on
    crusty bread slices
This recipe can easily be doubled for a party
    using an entire 14-oz (400-mL) can
    unsweetened coconut milk.
Makes: 6 appetizer servings

PREPARATION: 10 MINUTES
COOKING: 10 MINUTES

MAKE AHEAD: Stir sauce together and refrigerate for up to 2 days before cooking.

GARLIC SHRIMP WITH RED PEPPERS

Slow cooking mellows both the garlic and chilies in this fast stir-fry.
It's easy enough to do on a weeknight when you want to splurge.

In a large frying pan, heat
    2 tbsp butter
Add
    4 minced garlic cloves or 2 tsp bottled
       minced garlic
    ½ tsp hot red pepper flakes
Sauté over low heat until fragrant, about
    8 minutes. Increase heat to high and stir in
    1 julienned red pepper
Stir often for about 3 minutes, then stir in
    ¼ cup white wine

Add
    1 lb (500 g) fresh or frozen cooked
       or uncooked shelled shrimp
    4 sliced green onions
Stir constantly until shrimp are bright pink
    and hot, from 4 to 8 minutes.
Serve over orzo, fettuccine or rice.
    Makes: 4 to 6 first courses or 2 main courses

PREPARATION: 19 MINUTES
COOKING: 15 MINUTES

GARLIC SHRIMP WITH RED PEPPERS

APPETIZERS ◆ Hot

BAKED CHILI-GARLIC SHRIMP

Shrimp gets a jolt of taste from lime and garlic in this easy appetizer.

Preheat oven to 400°F (200°C). Remove shells, leaving tail attached, on
    1 lb (500 g) fresh or frozen uncooked large shrimp or large sea scallops
If using scallops, discard any small opaque pieces on sides. Place seafood in a single layer, in a shallow dish such as a 10-inch (25-cm) pie plate.
In a small pan, heat
    2 tbsp butter
Add
    4 minced garlic cloves
    2 tbsp freshly squeezed lime juice
    ½ tsp hot red pepper flakes
    ¼ tsp salt
Stir for 2 minutes. Pour over seafood. Stir until coated. Bake in preheated oven, uncovered, until shrimp are pink, or scallops are just firm, about 12 minutes.
Serve as a first course over rounds of
    crisp garlic toast or rice
Scatter with
    sliced green onions, chives or coriander
    Makes: 6 appetizer servings

> *PREPARATION: 15 MINUTES*
> *COOKING: 2 MINUTES*
> *BAKING: 12 MINUTES*

CAYENNE CRAB CAKES

This signature dish from Barbara-Jo McIntosh comes from her book Tin Fish Gourmet *(Raincoast Books).*

In a bowl, whisk together
    1 egg
    2 tbsp tomato paste
    1 tsp lemon juice
Stir in
    2 tbsp grated Parmesan
    2 finely chopped green onions
    1 tbsp finely chopped fresh coriander
    ¼ tsp cayenne
Then stir in
    2 tbsp all-purpose flour
    3 (4-oz/113-g) cans drained flaked crabmeat
Form rounded teaspoonfuls or tablespoonfuls into 30 to 40 patties. Coat each patty in all-purpose flour
Place on waxed paper. In a large frying pan, heat
    1½ tsp each butter and olive oil
Sauté cakes in batches over medium heat until lightly golden, from 3 to 5 minutes per side. Keep warm in a 200°F (90°C) oven while frying remaining patties, adding more butter and oil as needed. For dipping sauce, stir together
    ½ cup light mayonnaise
    ½ tsp cayenne
Serve with warm or room-temperature crab cakes.
    Makes: 30 to 40 small cakes

> *PREPARATION: 20 MINUTES*
> *COOKING: 30 MINUTES*

MAKE AHEAD: Freeze cooked crab cakes in a single layer on a baking sheet, then transfer to an airtight container or seal in plastic bag for up to a month. Reheat frozen cakes, uncovered, on baking sheet in 400°F (200°C) oven, from 9 to 12 minutes. Cayenne mayonnaise, covered, keeps at least a week in the refrigerator.

ST. JOHN'S COD CAKES

*These moist and succulent cod cakes are the creations of Françoise and
René Enguehard of St. John's, Newfoundland.*

Cut into large cubes
  1½ lbs (750 g) uncooked cod, haddock
    or halibut fillets
Whirl in a food processor until coarsely ground,
  then place in a bowl. Stir in
  1 finely chopped small onion
  1 minced garlic clove
  2 tbsp chopped fresh parsley
    or snipped chives
  ¼ tsp salt
Shape into 16 to 20 cakes, about 1½ inches
  (4 cm) wide. Coat each cake in
  all-purpose flour

In a large frying pan, heat
  2 tbsp vegetable oil
Sauté cakes in batches until golden, about
  3 minutes per side, adding more oil if needed.
Serve with mayonnaise spiked with lemon juice
  and chopped fresh dill or chives for dipping.
  Makes: 16 to 20 small fish cakes

  PREPARATION: 15 MINUTES
  COOKING: 18 MINUTES

ST. JOHN'S COD CAKES

MUSSELS IN BLACK BEAN SAUCE

*It would be hard to find an easier way to add an exotic-tasting sauce
to inexpensive mussels.*

Scrub under cold water and remove any
   beards from
   5 lbs (2.5 kg) mussels
Discard any mussels that are open and will
   not close when gently tapped. In a large
   wide saucepan, heat
   1 tbsp dark sesame oil
   2 tbsp finely chopped fresh ginger
     or 1 tbsp bottled minced ginger
   1 minced garlic clove
Cook, stirring until very fragrant, about
   1 minute. Stir in
   1 cup chicken broth or bouillon
   2 tbsp black bean sauce
   ¼ tsp chili-garlic sauce
     or hot red pepper flakes

Increase heat to medium-high. When bubbly,
   add mussels. Cover tightly and steam,
   stirring once, until mussels open, from 6 to
   8 minutes. Discard mussels that aren't open.
   Remove from heat. Using a slotted spoon,
   remove mussels to wide soup bowls, letting
   juice drip back into sauce in pan.
In a small bowl, stir together
   2 tbsp cold water
   2 tbsp cornstarch
Stir into sauce and place pan back on heat. Cook,
   stirring constantly, until thickened slightly,
   from 4 to 5 minutes. Pour over mussels and
   sprinkle with
   2 thinly sliced green onions
Serve with crusty bread to dip into broth.

Makes: 4 to 6 first courses or 2 main courses

PREPARATION: 10 MINUTES
COOKING: 13 MINUTES

Mussels in Black Bean Sauce

MUSSELS WITH TOMATO SALSA

*For a great inexpensive seafood starter,
pair mussels with fresh tomatoes.*

Scrub under cold water and remove any beards
   from
   4 lbs (2 kg) mussels
Discard any mussels that are open and will not
   close when gently tapped. In a large wide
   saucepan over medium-high heat, combine
   1 cup white wine
   1 small chopped red onion
   2 large minced garlic cloves
   ½ tsp hot red pepper flakes
Boil, uncovered and stirring often. When wine
   just covers bottom of pan after about
   5 minutes, stir in
   4 large chopped tomatoes
   1 tsp ground cumin
Add mussels. Cover and reduce heat to
   medium. Steam, stirring once until mussels
   are opened, from 6 to 8 minutes. Discard
   mussels that aren't open. Sprinkle with
   squeeze of lime or lemon juice
   2 thinly sliced green onions
   ¼ cup chopped fresh coriander or parsley
Serve with bread to dip into broth.
   Makes: 4 first courses or 2 main courses

   PREPARATION: 15 MINUTES
   COOKING: 13 MINUTES

SMOKED SALMON BRUSCHETTA

*This elegant appetizer can be made with smoked
salmon bits, available at a fraction of the cost of slices.*

Preheat oven to 400°F (200°C).
Stir together
   ¼ cup light sour cream
   2 tbsp chopped fresh dill
      or ¼ tsp dried dillweed
   pinch of white pepper
Stir in
   ½ lb (250 g) chopped smoked salmon
   4 thinly sliced green onions
Stir together
   ¼ cup melted butter or olive oil
   2 minced garlic cloves
Brush over both sides of
   1 baguette, cut into ½-inch (1-cm) thick slices
Place on a baking sheet and bake in preheated
   oven until golden, about 8 minutes. Spread
   with salmon mixture.
Garnish with fresh dill or sliced green onions.
   Mixture is also great on cucumber slices.
   Makes: 2 cups for 24 canapés

   PREPARATION: 15 MINUTES
   BAKING: 8 MINUTES

MAKE AHEAD: Salmon mixture keeps
well for a day in the refrigerator.

APPETIZERS ◆ Hot

APPETIZERS ◆ Hot

HOT MEXICAN PINWHEELS

For your next casual get-together, whip up these rolls and store in the refrigerator.

In a small bowl, stir together
  1/4 cup room-temperature or spreadable
    cream cheese
  1/2 cup grated mozzarella
  1 tbsp finely chopped pimento
  2 tsp finely chopped jalapeños
  1 finely chopped small green onion
Spread about 2 tablespoons over each of
  4 tortillas, about 7 inches (18 cm) wide
Roll up, wrap with plastic wrap and refrigerate
  for at least 2 hours or up to 3 days. Preheat
  oven to 425°F (220°C). Remove plastic wrap.
  Slice rolls into 1-inch (2.5-cm) rounds. Place
  on a baking sheet, seam-side down, and bake
  for 5 minutes.
Serve with salsa.
  Makes: 24 appetizers

PREPARATION: 10 MINUTES
BAKING: 5 MINUTES

MAKE AHEAD: Rolls will keep well
for at least 3 days in refrigerator.

Hot Mexican Pinwheels

MICROWAVE MEXICAN EGG ROLLS

Greet guests at your next brunch with mugs of coffee and a plate of these substantial appetizers.

In a microwave-safe dish, stir together
  1 chopped seeded green pepper
  1/2 cup salsa
  1/2 tsp each chili powder and ground cumin
Cover with plastic wrap, venting one corner.
  In another dish or large measuring cup,
  whisk together
  8 eggs
  3 tbsp water
  1/4 to 1/2 tsp hot pepper sauce
  1/4 tsp each salt and black pepper
Microwave salsa mixture on high for 2 minutes,
  then remove. Microwave eggs on high,
  uncovered, for 4½ minutes, stirring every
  30 seconds. Then microwave
  6 tortillas, about 7 inches (18 cm) wide
  on a paper towel-lined plate, 30 seconds.
  Heap eggs into centre of warm tortillas,
  spoon a little warm salsa over each, then
  sprinkle with
  grated Monterey Jack or cheddar, about
    1½ cups total
Dot each with about
  2 tbsp sour cream, about ¾ cup total
Top with
  shredded lettuce, about 2 cups total
Roll up and gently slice in half or thirds.
  Makes: 12 appetizers or 3 breakfast entrées

PREPARATION: 15 MINUTES
MICROWAVING: 7 MINUTES

Mini Light Italian Meatballs

Serve these calorie-light chicken meatballs with a bowl of salsa or dilled sour cream for dipping.

Preheat oven to 375°F (190°C). In a small frying pan, melt
    2 tbsp butter
Add
    1 finely chopped onion
    1 finely chopped celery stalk
Sauté until soft, 5 minutes. In a large bowl, whisk together
    2 eggs
    1/4 cup sour cream
    2 tbsp Dijon
    1/2 tsp Italian seasonings
    1/4 tsp each nutmeg, salt and pepper
Stir in onions and celery.
Add
    2 lbs (1 kg) ground chicken or turkey
    1 1/2 cups store-bought dry bread crumbs
Blend well. Shape into small balls, about 1 inch (2.5 cm) wide. Place in a single layer on lightly oiled baking sheets. Bake in preheated oven, uncovered, until lightly browned and no longer pink in the middle, about 15 minutes.
Makes: 78 small meatballs

> *PREPARATION: 30 MINUTES*
> *COOKING: 5 MINUTES*
> *BAKING: 15 MINUTES*

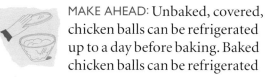

MAKE AHEAD: Unbaked, covered, chicken balls can be refrigerated up to a day before baking. Baked chicken balls can be refrigerated for 2 days or frozen. Reheat in the microwave.

Classy Curried Meatballs

Jacqueline Lee Guisso of Bramalea raves about these meatballs created by her mother, Sharon Lee.

Preheat oven to 350°F (180°C). In a large bowl, work together until well mixed
    2 lbs (1 kg) lean ground beef
    1 beaten egg
    3 tbsp curry powder
    1 tsp salt
    1/2 tsp freshly ground black pepper
    3/4 cup store-bought dry bread crumbs
    or 1 1/2 cups fresh bread crumbs
Roll into 3/4 inch (1.5 cm) balls. Cook in batches without crowding in an oiled frying pan, until lightly browned, from 5 to 8 minutes. Remove to a 9x13-inch (3-L) baking pan. Pour over top
    18-oz (455-mL) bottle barbecue sauce
Cover with foil. Bake in centre of preheated oven until hot and bubbly, from 25 to 30 minutes. Sprinkle with chopped fresh parsley.
Makes: 70 meatballs

> *PREPARATION: 30 MINUTES*
> *COOKING: 20 MINUTES*
> *BAKING: 25 MINUTES*

MAKE AHEAD: Bake meatballs in sauce, then cover and refrigerate for up to 2 days or freeze. Reheat in a covered pan over medium-low heat or in a covered dish at 350°F (180°C) or microwave on medium, stirring often.

APPETIZERS ◆ Hot

SPICY SWEET 'N' SOUR MEATBALLS

*This recipe with grape jelly in the sauce has been
a favorite of meatball lovers for years.*

Preheat oven to 350°F (180°C). In a large bowl,
whisk together
2 eggs
1 tsp horseradish
½ tsp each salt and black pepper
Crumble in
1½ lbs (750 g) medium ground beef
½ lb (250 g) ground pork, veal or chicken
½ cup store-bought dry bread crumbs
Blend well, shape into 1-inch (2.5-cm) balls and
place slightly apart on greased baking sheets
with shallow sides. Bake in centre of
preheated oven, turning every 5 minutes,
until lightly browned, from 10 to 15 minutes.
Meanwhile, in a large saucepan, combine
1 finely chopped onion
1 minced garlic clove
½ cup each water, grape jelly, ketchup
and chili sauce
¼ cup each brown sugar and cider vinegar
1 tbsp Worcestershire
1 tsp dry mustard
¼ tsp hot pepper sauce
Bring to a boil, stirring often, then reduce heat
and simmer, uncovered, 5 minutes. Add
baked meatballs and simmer, stirring often,
5 minutes.
Makes: 84 meatballs

PREPARATION: 25 MINUTES
BAKING: 15 MINUTES
COOKING: 10 MINUTES

MAKE AHEAD: Refrigerate baked
meatballs in sauce for up to 2 days
or freeze. Reheat over low heat
or in microwave. Or freeze
browned meatballs, then add frozen to
sauce and simmer until hot.

SASSY SALSA MEATBALLS

*Mexican flavors abound in these moist
chili-scented meatballs with a creamy salsa dip.*

Preheat oven to 400°F (200°C). In a large mixing
bowl, whisk together until blended
2 eggs
1 cup very thick salsa
Stir in
2 tsp chili powder
½ tsp each salt and freshly ground
black pepper
1 cup finely crushed tortilla or corn chips
Work in
2 lbs (1 kg) medium ground beef
1 cup chopped fresh coriander
4 thinly sliced green onions
Roll into 1-inch (2.5-cm) balls. Place slightly
apart on greased baking pans with shallow
sides. Bake in centre of preheated oven,
uncovered, until browned, from 15 to
18 minutes, turning once. Stir together
1 cup each salsa and sour cream
Stir in hot meatballs or sprinkle meatballs
with chopped fresh coriander and use
sauce for dipping.
Makes: 80 meatballs

PREPARATION: 20 MINUTES
BAKING: 18 MINUTES

MAKE AHEAD: Place entire pans of
baked meatballs in freezer. When
frozen, place meatballs in plastic
bags and seal. Keep frozen for up to
a month. Reheat frozen meatballs in microwave
or in a preheated 350°F (180°C) oven for
about 15 minutes.

SOUTHERN TORTILLA WEDGES

Tortilla triangles topped with beans, salsa and sour cream are great for an informal relaxed gathering.

In a saucepan, heat
    14-oz (398-mL) can refried beans
    ¼ cup salsa
Stir often over medium heat until hot and
    bubbly, about 5 minutes. Or microwave,
    covered, on high, 2 minutes. Stir in
    4 thinly sliced green onions
In a preheated 400°F (200°C) oven,
    warm for 4 minutes
    6 tortillas, about 7 inches (18 cm) wide

Slice each tortilla into 4 wedges. Spoon about
    1 tablespoon of hot bean mixture into centre
    of wedges. Top with
    dollops of sour cream, about ¾ cup total
Add
    a thin slice of avocado or sprig of coriander
Makes: 24 wedges

PREPARATION: 15 MINUTES
COOKING: 5 MINUTES

SOUTHERN TORTILLA WEDGES

CRISPY HOT TACO FINGERS

Kids of all ages adore these terrific "chip" fingers – perfect for when friends drop by.

Preheat oven to 375°F (190°C). Finely crush
  8-oz (225-g) bag taco chips
Place in a wide shallow plate. In a bowl,
  whisk together
  2 eggs
  ¼ cup hot salsa
  ¼ to ½ tsp hot pepper sauce
Cut into 1½ x 3-inch (3.5 x 7-cm) fingers
  1 lb (500 g) skinless, boneless chicken breasts

Dip into egg mixture, then roll in crushed
  chips. Place slightly apart on a wire rack set
  on a shallow-sided baking sheet. Bake in
  preheated oven until lightly browned, from
  15 to 20 minutes. Serve with dips such as
  salsa, guacamole and sour cream, flavored
  with chopped fresh coriander.
Makes: 20 fingers

PREPARATION: 20 MINUTES
BAKING: 20 MINUTES

MAKE AHEAD: Prepare fingers and
refrigerate, uncovered, for up to a
day. Then bake. Baked fingers can be
refrigerated for a day or frozen.
Reheat, uncovered, in a 350°F (180°C) oven.
Use mild salsa and omit pepper sauce for
people who don't like it too hot.

JAZZY CAESAR CHICKEN FINGERS

All the great tastes of a Caesar salad join forces in the creamy coating of these crisp breaded nibblers.

Preheat oven to 450°F (230°C). Cut into ½-inch
  (1-cm) wide strips
  2 lbs (1 kg) skinless, boneless chicken breasts
Toss in
  ¾ cup creamy Caesar dressing
In a medium-size bowl, stir together
  4 cups fresh bread crumbs (about 8 slices
    crumbled) or 2 cups store-bought dry
    bread crumbs
  ½ cup chopped cooked bacon
    or ¼ cup simulated bacon bits (optional)
  ¼ cup freshly grated Parmesan
  ¼ cup finely chopped parsley
  ¼ tsp each salt and ground black pepper
Roll coated strips in crumbs and place on a wire
  rack set on a greased baking sheet. Bake in
  centre of preheated oven until lightly
  browned, about 15 minutes.
Serve warm with additional Caesar dressing
  for dipping.
Makes: 48 fingers

PREPARATION: 20 MINUTES
BAKING: 15 MINUTES

MAKE AHEAD: Bake chicken for
12 minutes. Cool, wrap in foil and
freeze. Reheat right from the
freezer, uncovered, in a preheated
350°F (180°C) oven until hot and crisp,
about 12 minutes.

Sweet 'n' Sour Chicken Balls

This healthy version of a Chinese food favorite is perfect with Sweet 'n' Sour Sauce (see recipe right).

In a large bowl, mix together
  1 lb (500 g) ground chicken or turkey
  1 beaten egg
  3 thinly sliced green onions
  ½ tsp salt
  ¼ tsp cayenne
Stir in
  2 cups soft fresh bread crumbs
Shape into 1-inch (2.5-cm) balls.
  In a large nonstick frying pan, heat
  1 tbsp vegetable oil
Add about half of the chicken balls. Do not crowd pan. Shake pan often to brown chicken balls on all sides, from 8 to 10 minutes. Remove and repeat with remaining balls, adding more oil if needed. Then shake
  1 cup Sweet 'n' Sour Sauce (see recipe right)
Add to pan. Stir often until sauce is bubbly and clear, about 5 minutes. Then return all meatballs to sauce and stir often until meatballs are hot.
Serve with toothpicks.
  Makes: 30 meatballs

  PREPARATION: 20 MINUTES
  COOKING: 15 MINUTES

Sweet 'n' Sour Sauce

Shake up a jar of this sauce in 5 minutes for Sweet 'n' Sour Chicken Balls (see recipe left).

In a large jar, stir together until fairly smooth
  ⅓ cup cornstarch
  ½ cup granulated sugar
  ¼ cup white or rice wine vinegar
  2 tbsp soy sauce
Add
  2 cups chicken bouillon or broth
  2 minced garlic cloves
    or ½ tsp garlic powder
  1 tbsp finely grated fresh ginger
    or ½ tsp ground ginger
  ¼ tsp hot red pepper flakes (optional)
Shake vigorously. Seal and refrigerate for up to 1 week. To use, shake jar and heat desired amount in a small saucepan or microwave, stirring often, until bubbly and clear.
  Makes: 3 cups

  PREPARATION: 10 MINUTES

Sweet 'n' Sour Chicken Balls

OVEN CHICKEN NUGGETS

*Make your own golden nuggets for a fraction of
the cost – and fat – of store-bought.*

Preheat oven to 400°F (200°C). Oil an 8-inch
    (2-L) baking dish with
    I tbsp vegetable oil
Cut into 8 nugget-sized pieces
    2 large skinless, boneless chicken breasts
In a wide shallow bowl, beat together
    I egg
    3 tbsp regular or 2% evaporated milk
        or light cream
In another bowl, stir together
    ¾ cup store-bought dry bread crumbs
    ¼ cup grated Parmesan
    ¼ tsp salt
    ¼ tsp cayenne (optional)
    pinch of dried oregano
In a small dish, sprinkle
    ¼ cup all-purpose flour
Dip each nugget into flour, then egg mixture
    and finally into bread crumbs. If you like a
    thick coating, double-dip chicken pieces
    in egg and crumbs. Arrange nuggets slightly
    apart in oiled dish. Bake in preheated
    oven for 15 minutes. Turn nuggets and
    continue baking until golden and crisp,
    10 to 15 more minutes.
Serve warm with barbecue, salsa or spaghetti
    sauce for dipping.
    Makes: 14 to 16 nuggets

*PREPARATION: 20 MINUTES
BAKING: 30 MINUTES*

SATYR'S SKEWERS & PEANUT SAUCE

*Therese Taylor uses generous splashes of her Dan T's
hot sauce for this superb peanut dipping sauce.*

For Spiced Cayenne Sauce: In a large frying pan
    over medium-high, heat
    I tbsp vegetable oil
Add
    I finely chopped onion
    2 large minced garlic cloves
Sauté for 5 minutes. Stir in
    I cup chicken broth
    ⅓ cup smooth or crunchy peanut butter
    I to 4 tbsp hot pepper sauce such as Dan T's
        Spiced Cayenne Sauce
Bring to a boil, then reduce heat and simmer,
    uncovered and stirring often, about
    5 minutes. Remove from heat and stir in
    I tbsp finely chopped fresh coriander
For skewers: Cut into bite-size pieces
    I lb (500 g) skinless, boneless chicken breasts
In a large frying pan over medium-high, heat
    I tbsp olive oil
Sauté chicken, stirring often, until golden, from
    6 to 8 minutes. Stir in
    I tbsp freshly squeezed lime or lemon juice
    I tsp hot sauce
    pinches of salt and cumin
Serve chicken on skewers with
    room-temperature sauce.
    Makes: 24 skewers and 1½ cups sauce

*PREPARATION: 15 MINUTES
COOKING: 18 MINUTES*

MAKE AHEAD: Sauce will keep in
refrigerator, covered, for several
days. Cooked chicken will keep
in refrigerator for a day. Warm
chicken in microwave or oven.

CHÈVRE TORTE

Chef Glenys Morgan created this creamy appetizer for the cookbook
The Girls Who Dish: Top Women Chefs Cook Their Best *(Whitecap, 1998).*

Preheat oven to 350°F (180°C). Generously coat inside of an 8½-inch (22-cm) springform pan with butter. In a food processor, whirl until finely ground
½ cup store-bought dry bread crumbs
3 tbsp chopped hazelnuts

Turn into buttered pan. Rotate to coat sides up to a height of about 1 inch (2.5 cm). In a food processor, whirl together
4.5 oz (140 g) chèvre roll, about 1¼ cups
8-oz (250-g) pkg light or regular cream cheese

Add and whirl
3 eggs
2 small minced garlic cloves

2 to 3 tbsp chopped fresh basil, chives or tarragon
¼ tsp each salt and black pepper

Pour over crumbs and spread evenly. Bake in centre of preheated oven until centre seems firm when pan is jiggled, from 35 to 40 minutes. Cool at least 10 minutes before removing sides.

Serve warm wedges topped with salsa (see Mango & Sweet Pepper Salsa, page 59). Torte will keep well, covered and refrigerated, for at least 2 days.
Makes: 10 to 12 servings

PREPARATION: 15 MINUTES
BAKING: 40 MINUTES

CHÈVRE TORTE

CHEESE 'N' BACON CANAPÉS

A winning flavor combo gets uptown treatment in this appetizer.

Preheat oven to 400°F (200°C). In a frying pan, arrange
  8 bacon slices

Cook bacon over medium-high heat, turning once, until lightly browned and crisp, about 5 minutes. Transfer to a plate lined with paper towels to absorb fat. When cool enough to handle, crumble or chop bacon and place in a medium-size bowl. Stir in
  2 cups grated old cheddar
  8 oz (250 g) room-temperature cream cheese
  ½ tsp Worcestershire
  ½ cup slivered almonds

Cut crusts from
  15 slices white bread

Spread slices with cheese mixture. Cut into quarters. Arrange on a baking sheet. Bake in preheated oven until golden, from 8 to 10 minutes.
Makes: 5 dozen

PREPARATION: 20 MINUTES
COOKING: 10 MINUTES

MAKE AHEAD: Place uncooked canapés on a baking sheet. Place in freezer, uncovered, until frozen. Place in freezer bags and seal. When ready to use, bake frozen canapés in a preheated 375°F (190°C) oven from 10 to 12 minutes, until piping hot and golden.

WARM PEARS 'N' CHEESE

Add a warm welcome to your meal with this sophisticated starter that takes only 10 minutes.

Preheat broiler. Cut in half lengthwise and core
  4 firm unpeeled ripe pears

Without cutting through stem end, make several thin slices lengthwise from wide-rounded bottom. Separate slices slightly to form a fan and place on baking sheet. Top each with a slice of
  Gorgonzola, Cambozola or Camembert cheese, cut ¼ inch (0.5 cm) thick, about 8 oz (250 g) total

Broil just until cheese melts, about 1 minute. Place on small plates. Sprinkle with
  fresh mint leaves

Serve with
  baguette slices
Makes: 8 appetizers

PREPARATION: 10 MINUTES
BROILING: 1 MINUTE

INSTANT QUESADILLAS

For nibbles in a hurry, use a package of tortillas and spread and sprinkle with these trendy toppings.

Lightly spread
  2 tortillas, about 7 inches (18 cm) wide
with
  Dijon

Sprinkle with
  ⅔ cup grated old cheddar
  2 tbsp sliced green onion
  2 tbsp chopped fresh coriander

Roll snugly. Wrap with plastic wrap. Microwave 40 to 50 seconds. Or wrap in foil and bake at 350°F (180°C) for 12 minutes.

Slice into pieces and serve with salsa.
Makes: 12 pieces

PREPARATION: 5 MINUTES
BAKING: 12 MINUTES

BRIE & WALNUT MUSHROOMS

These hot, stuffed mushroom caps are incredibly sophisticated and incredibly easy to make.

Preheat oven to 375°F (190°C). In a food
  processor, whirl until fairly smooth
  6 oz (185 g) Brie cheese, cut into cubes
  ½ cup coarsely chopped walnuts
Spoon mixture into about
  30 large mushroom caps
Place caps on a baking sheet in preheated
  oven just until hot, about 5 minutes.
  Makes: 1 cup filling for about
  30 mushroom caps

> *PREPARATION: 5 MINUTES*
> *BAKING: 5 MINUTES*

MAKE AHEAD: Brie and nut mixture
will keep well for at least 3 days in
refrigerator.

CHIC CHÈVRE TOMATOES

These grilled tomatoes are great for an appetizer buffet.

Slice in half
  4 ripe round or plum tomatoes
Gently squeeze out seeds and juice. Place cut-
  side up on a baking sheet. Crumble over top
  herbed goat cheese
Sprinkle with
  finely chopped fresh basil and garlic chives
Grill several inches below preheated broiler until
  cheese is hot, about 5 minutes.
  Makes: 8 halves

> *PREPARATION: 5 MINUTES*
> *BAKING: 5 MINUTES*

CHIC CHÈVRE TOMATOES

BREADS

Five grains, including cornmeal and bran, give healthy country goodness to this FAST MULTIGRAIN BREAD *(see recipe page 38).*

BREADS

FAST MULTIGRAIN BREAD

This bread takes a little longer to make, but its mix of many grains makes it worth the effort.

In a large bowl, stir together
   1 cup whole-wheat flour
   1 cup rye flour
   1 cup natural bran
   1/2 cup cornmeal
   1/3 cup brown sugar
   3 tsp salt
   1/2 tsp cinnamon (optional)
   1 pkg instant yeast
     or about 1 tbsp regular yeast
Make a well in centre. Whisk together
   1 cup milk
   1 cup water
   1/4 cup olive oil
Heat in microwave or a saucepan until hot, but not boiling. Pour into well and stir just until combined. Work in
   1 1/2 cups all-purpose flour
Turn out onto a floured board. Knead 10 minutes. As dough becomes sticky, work in more flour as needed, up to
   1 1/2 cups all-purpose flour
Form dough into a ball and let rest 10 minutes. Form into 2 oval loaves about 2 inches (5 cm) high and place on a greased baking sheet. Cover with greased waxed paper and a damp towel. Let rise until doubled, about 1 hour. Uncover and bake in preheated 350°F (180°C) oven until bread sounds hollow when bottom is tapped, about 50 minutes.
Makes: 2 small loaves

PREPARATION: 30 MINUTES
RESTING: 10 MINUTES
RISING: 1 HOUR
BAKING: 50 MINUTES

WHOLE-WHEAT CORN BREAD

Whole-wheat flour gives a rustic wholesomeness to this corn bread – perfect with chili or chicken.

Preheat oven to 375°F (190°C). Butter or coat with cooking spray a 9x5-inch (2-L) loaf pan. Stir together
   1 1/2 cups cornmeal
   2 cups milk
Let soak while assembling other ingredients.
   In a bowl, stir together
   1 cup all-purpose flour
   1 cup whole-wheat flour
   1/4 cup granulated sugar
   2 tbsp baking powder
   1 tsp salt
In a large bowl, whisk together
   2 eggs
   1/4 cup olive or vegetable oil
Fold in cornmeal mixture. Add
   1/2 cup finely chopped sun-dried tomatoes
   (optional)
Stir in flour mixture. Turn into prepared pan, smooth top and bake in centre of preheated oven until a skewer inserted into centre comes out clean, about 1 1/4 hours. Cool in pan for 5 minutes before turning out. Serve warm or cool completely, then wrap. Store at room temperature for 1 to 2 days or cover and freeze.
Makes: 18 (1/2-inch/1-cm) slices

PREPARATION: 10 MINUTES
BAKING: 1 1/4 HOURS

SESAME CORN BREAD

Wheat germ and sesame seeds add a "nutty" texture and fibre boost to stir-together corn bread.

Preheat oven to 375°F (190°C). Butter an 8-inch (2-L) square pan. In a bowl, whisk together

    2 eggs
    1 cup milk
    ⅓ cup vegetable oil

In a large bowl, stir together

    1 cup all-purpose flour
    1 cup yellow cornmeal
    ⅓ cup wheat germ
    ¼ cup toasted sesame or sunflower seeds
    2 tbsp granulated sugar
    3 tsp baking powder
    ¼ tsp salt

Make a well in centre. Pour in egg mixture and stir just until combined. Turn into buttered pan and smooth top. Bake in centre of preheated oven until a skewer inserted into centre comes out clean, from 25 to 30 minutes. Cut into 16 squares. Great warm. Store at room temperature for a day or cover and freeze.

Makes: 16 squares

PREPARATION: 15 MINUTES
BAKING: 30 MINUTES

HERBED WHOLE-WHEAT SODA BREAD

The unique taste of this country soda bread is unrivaled and a great companion for cheddar.

Preheat oven to 400°F (200°C). In a large bowl, stir together

    2 cups all-purpose flour
    1¾ cups whole-wheat flour
    1½ tsp caraway seeds (optional)
    1 tsp each baking soda, dried basil, dried
      leaf thyme, dried leaf oregano and salt

Using fingers, rub in

    ¼ cup cold butter

until crumbly, but tiny pieces of butter can still be seen. Make a well in centre. Stir in

    1¾ cups buttermilk or low-fat yogurt

On a greased baking sheet, form into a flat round loaf about 8 inches (20 cm) across. Cut a ½-inch (1-cm) deep cross into top. Bake until a skewer inserted into centre comes out clean, from 45 to 55 minutes. Cool. Store at room temperature for 2 days or cover and freeze.

Makes: 12 wedges

PREPARATION: 10 MINUTES
BAKING: 55 MINUTES

Sesame Corn Bread

BREADS

DILLED BUTTERMILK BREAD

*Serve thick slices of this warm bread with
soup to sop up all the juicy goodness.*

Preheat oven to 350°F (180°C). Butter a 9x5-inch
(2-L) loaf pan. In a large bowl, stir together
   2 cups all-purpose flour
   2 tsp baking powder
   ½ tsp each baking soda and salt
   ¼ tsp black pepper
When blended, stir in
   ½ cup chopped fresh dill
      or 1 tbsp dried dillweed
   ⅓ cup toasted sesame seeds (optional)
Make a well in centre. In another bowl,
   whisk together
   1 egg
   1¼ cups buttermilk
   ¼ cup melted butter
Pour into well and stir until just combined.
   Turn into buttered pan and smooth top.
   Sprinkle with additional sesame seeds. Bake
   in centre of preheated oven until a skewer
   inserted into centre comes out clean, from
   60 to 65 minutes. Cool in pan for 5 minutes
   before turning out on a rack. Store at room
   temperature for 2 days or cover and freeze.
Makes: 18 (½-inch/1-cm) slices

*PREPARATION: 15 MINUTES
BAKING: 65 MINUTES*

LEMON-PEPPER BREAD

*Serve this zesty loaf with tuna or salmon salad or
with entrées such as grilled salmon steak.*

Preheat oven to 350°F (180°C). Butter a
   9x5-inch (2-L) loaf pan. In a large bowl,
   stir together
   2 cups all-purpose flour
   ½ cup granulated sugar
   2 tsp baking powder
   ¾ tsp freshly ground black pepper
   ½ tsp each baking soda and salt
Stir in
   finely grated peel of 1 lemon
Make a well in centre. In another bowl,
   whisk together
   1 egg
   1 cup milk
   ⅓ cup melted butter
   5 tbsp freshly squeezed lemon juice
Immediately pour into flour mixture. Stir until
   evenly mixed. Turn into buttered pan and
   smooth top. Bake in centre of preheated oven
   until a skewer inserted into centre comes out
   clean, about 1 hour. Cool in pan 5 minutes
   before turning out on a rack. Store bread
   at room temperature for a day or cover
   and freeze.
Makes: 18 (½-inch/1-cm) slices

*PREPARATION: 15 MINUTES
BAKING: 1 HOUR*

Lemon-Pepper Bread

INDIAN CHAPATI BREAD

Freshly made chapati bread, the basic bread of India, is a smooth, pliable, thin round of flatbread.

In a large bowl, stir together
  2 cups whole-wheat flour
  1 cup all-purpose flour
  ½ tsp salt
Slowly stir in until a dough forms
  1¼ cups water
Gather dough into a ball. Sprinkle a little flour on counter and place dough on top. Knead until stiff and difficult to work, about 3 minutes, sprinkling extra flour over counter when dough becomes sticky. Divide dough into 10 pieces and rest, covered with plastic wrap for 15 minutes.

Then, using a floured rolling pin on a floured surface, roll one piece into a 6- to 7-inch (15- to 18-cm) circle. Sprinkle each side with flour. Repeat, stacking rounds and covering with plastic. Heat a large oiled cast-iron pan or griddle over medium heat until piping hot. Meanwhile, roll one round into a thinner 9- to 10-inch (23- to 25-cm) circle. Cook until side in contact with pan is flecked with brown spots, about 1 minute. Flip and cook the other side, about 1 minute. Repeat rolling and frying of each round, stacking in a folded kitchen towel to keep warm.

Serve warm with Easy Antipasto or Curried Chili Dip (see recipes pages 12 and 50).

Makes: 10 thin rounds

PREPARATION: 35 MINUTES
COOKING: 2 MINUTES PER ROUND

MAKE AHEAD: Cook chapatis and store at room temperature for up to a day. Reheat each round in an ungreased hot skillet for 30 seconds or separated by paper towels in a microwave.

CURRIED GARLIC STICKS

Serve these crusty bold-flavored bread sticks with drinks, whether it's fine wine or beer.

Preheat oven to 450°F (230°C). In a small saucepan over very low heat, combine
  ¼ cup butter
  2 minced garlic cloves
    or 2 tsp bottled minced garlic
  1½ tsp curry powder
  ¼ tsp cayenne
Cover and simmer, stirring often, for 10 minutes. Meanwhile, in a large bowl, stir together
  2 cups all-purpose flour
  3 tsp baking powder
  ¾ tsp salt
Using a pastry cutter or two knives, cut in
  ¼ cup cold butter
  until the size of small peas. Make a well in centre. Add
  1 cup milk
Stir until dough leaves sides of bowl. Turn onto a floured surface and knead no more than 10 times. Pat into an 8-inch (20-cm) square. Cut in half, then cut each half into 8 sticks. Arrange ½ inch (1 cm) apart on a greased baking sheet with shallow sides. Brush with hot curry butter. Bake in centre of preheated oven until browned, from 12 to 15 minutes. Great hot with creamy dips or hot or cold soups.

Makes: 16 bread sticks

PREPARATION: 15 MINUTES
COOKING: 10 MINUTES
BAKING: 15 MINUTES

MAKE AHEAD: Bake bread sticks, then cool and wrap. Keep at room temperature for up to 2 days or freeze. Reheat, uncovered, in a 300°F (150°C) oven until hot, from 5 to 10 minutes.

BREADS

THREE-WAY BREAD STICKS

Follow three easy steps to make these freshly baked bread sticks at a fraction of the cost of store-bought.

Preheat oven to 375°F (190°C). For each topping, use
 1 lb (500 g) defrosted pizza or bread dough
Roll dough into a 12x10-inch (30x25-cm) rectangle. Spread or sprinkle with one topping. Cut into ¾-inch (2-cm) wide strips. Place about 2 inches (5 cm) apart on a greased baking sheet. Let rise, uncovered, at room temperature until doubled, about 30 minutes. Bake in centre of preheated oven until golden brown, about 20 minutes.
Makes: 42 bread sticks from 3 lbs dough

> *PREPARATION: 15 MINUTES*
> *RISING: 30 MINUTES*
> *BAKING: 20 MINUTES*

GARLIC BUTTER TOPPING
Stir 2 minced garlic cloves with 1 tsp Italian seasonings or ½ tsp each dried leaf oregano and basil and 2 tbsp room-temperature butter.

CHEDDAR & CHILI TOPPING
Toss 1½ cups grated old cheddar cheese with ½ tsp hot red pepper flakes.

CAESAR TOPPING
Stir ⅓ cup creamy Caesar dressing with ⅓ cup grated Parmesan and 1 tbsp chopped fresh parsley or 1 tsp dried parsley flakes.

MAKE AHEAD: Store baked cooled bread sticks at room temperature or refrigerate, covered, for up to 2 days or freeze. Reheat frozen bread sticks, uncovered, in a preheated 350°F (180°C) oven until warm, about 5 minutes.

MOROCCAN PITA CRISPS

Just a sprinkling of seasonings turns pita bread into exotic nibblers. Wonderful with creamy soups or dips.

Preheat oven to 350°F (180°C). In a small bowl, stir together
 ¼ cup olive oil or melted butter
 ½ tsp each curry powder and ground cumin
Split into 6 rounds
 3 (6-inch/15-cm) pita breads
Brush both sides with curry oil. Stack 2 or 3 pieces together and slice into 10 narrow wedges. Repeat with remaining pita. Scatter over an ungreased baking sheet in a single layer. Don't overlap. Bake in batches if necessary. Sprinkle with
 salt and freshly ground black pepper
Then bake until crisp, from 8 to 10 minutes. Great warm or at room temperature. Store in an airtight container.
Makes: 60 crisps

> *PREPARATION: 15 MINUTES*
> *BAKING: 10 MINUTES*

HOT GARLIC BREAD

Use these hot slices of chewy garlic bread in your salad or soup instead of the predictable croutons.

Place oven rack 4 inches (10 cm) from element and preheat broiler. Slice into 1-inch (2.5-cm) thick slices
 1 loaf crusty bread
Stir together
 ¼ to ⅓ cup room-temperature butter
 ¾ tsp garlic powder or 2 minced garlic cloves
 1 tsp dried parsley or chives
Thinly spread on both sides of each slice. Place garlic bread under broiler until bubbly and edges are golden, about 1 minute per side.
Makes: 10 thick slices

> *PREPARATION: 10 MINUTES*
> *BROILING: 2 MINUTES*

GOLDEN CORNMEAL MUFFINS

A hint of mace rounds out the full corn flavor in these picture-perfect muffins.
Serve them as an alternative to bread.

Preheat oven to 400°F (200°C). Generously grease 12 muffin cups. In a large bowl, using a fork, stir together

1½ cups cornmeal
1¾ cups all-purpose flour
2½ tsp baking powder
1½ tsp baking soda
¾ tsp ground mace
¾ tsp salt

In a small bowl, whisk together

2 eggs
2 cups buttermilk
¾ cup lightly packed brown sugar
¼ cup melted butter or vegetable oil

Stir into flour mixture just until combined. Some small lumps will remain. Spoon batter into muffin cups, filling to brims. Bake in centre of preheated oven until golden and a cake tester inserted into centre of a muffin comes out clean, from 15 to 18 minutes. Cool muffins in cups for 5 minutes, then turn out onto a cooling rack.
Makes: 12 muffins

> PREPARATION: 10 MINUTES
> BAKING: 18 MINUTES

GOLDEN CORNMEAL MUFFINS

BREADS

CHEDDAR-CHILI FOCACCIA

This cross between Italian flat bread and crusty pizza is a snap to make with pizza or bread dough.

Preheat oven to 400°F (200°C). Lightly grease a pizza pan or large baking sheet. Without trying to cover pan surface, evenly pat out until ½ inch (1 cm) thick
  1½ lbs (750 g) fresh or defrosted pizza or bread dough
Brush with
  1 tbsp olive oil
Sprinkle with
  ½ cup grated cheddar
  ½ tsp hot red pepper flakes
  ¼ tsp coarse salt or pinch of regular salt (optional)
Let rise, uncovered, until doubled, from 15 to 30 minutes. Using your index finger, poke holes in dough, about 1 inch (2.5 cm) apart, right down to, but not through, bottom. Bake in centre of preheated oven until golden, about 25 minutes. Slide bread off pan and onto a rack to cool.
Makes: 12 to 16 pieces

PREPARATION: 10 MINUTES
RISING: 30 MINUTES
BAKING: 25 MINUTES

VARIATION: ROSEMARY PARMESAN
Replace cheddar with ½ cup grated Parmesan. Omit hot red pepper flakes. Sprinkle with 1½ tsp crumbled rosemary or Italian seasonings.

REMARKABLY EASY FOCACCIA

You can turn bread dough into something special before baking by sprinkling with cheese or basil.

Preheat oven to 425°F (210°C). Pat
  1 lb (500 g) pizza or bread dough
into a greased 9x12-inch (23x28-cm) baking sheet. Let rise, covered, for 20 minutes. Using your index finger, poke holes in dough, about 1 inch (2.5 cm) apart, right down to but not through bottom. Combine
  2 tbsp olive oil
  2 crushed garlic cloves
Brush over dough. Sprinkle with
  ½ to 1 tsp dried rosemary
  ¼ tsp coarse salt
Bake in centre of preheated oven until golden, about 13 minutes.
Makes: 12 pieces

PREPARATION: 15 MINUTES
RISING: 20 MINUTES
BAKING: 13 MINUTES

SALSA PITA CRISPS

It's easy to turn that package of pita in your freezer into a bowl of crispy chips for scooping up salsa.

Preheat oven to 300°F (150°C). Lightly brush both sides of
  6 (6-inches/15-cm) pita breads
with
  1 tbsp olive oil
Cut each into 8 wedges. Open each triangle, splitting in half along curved edge. Spread out in a single layer on ungreased baking sheets. Bake in preheated oven, stirring occasionally, until lightly browned and crisp, about 20 minutes. Cool if not using immediately. Store in a tightly sealed bag at room temperature for up to 2 days.
Makes: 96 crisps

PREPARATION: 15 MINUTES
BAKING: 20 MINUTES

BARBECUED HERB-BUTTER BAGUETTE

Here's a fine garlic bread to heat on the barbecue.
Great for nibbling while the steaks sizzle.

In a small bowl, stir together
   ¼ cup room-temperature unsalted butter
   1 minced garlic clove
   ¼ tsp each freshly ground black pepper
      and dried leaf basil
   generous pinch of salt
Without cutting right through bottom, slice
   diagonally into 1-inch (2.5-cm) thick slices
   1 baguette
Lightly spread butter mixture on both sides of
   each slice. Retaining baguette's original
   shape, snugly wrap in foil. Grill on preheated
   barbecue for 15 minutes, turning halfway
   through. Or don't wrap, cut slices apart and
   grill individually on barbecue. Or warm
   in a 400°F (200°C) oven until piping hot
   or golden.
   Makes: 6 to 8 servings

PREPARATION: 15 MINUTES
BARBECUING: 15 MINUTES

 MAKE AHEAD: Prepare baguette, wrap
and store at room temperature for up
to a day before heating.

CHEDDAR CHEESE SCONES

Nippy cheddar and a pinch of cayenne give
character to these light-textured scones.

Preheat oven to 450°F (230°C). Grease a
   baking sheet. In a large bowl, using a fork,
   stir together
   2 cups all-purpose flour
   3 tsp baking powder
   ¾ tsp salt
   ½ tsp black pepper or ¼ tsp cayenne
Work in until crumbly
   ¼ cup cold butter, cubed
Stir in
   1 cup grated old cheddar
Make a well in centre. Stir in just until moistened
   1 cup cold milk
Turn onto a floured board. Divide in half and
   pat each into a 6-inch (15-cm) circle, about
   ¾ inch (2 cm) thick. Cut each into 6 wedges.
   Bake on greased sheet about 1 inch (2.5 cm)
   apart for crusty-sided scones or ½ inch
   (1 cm) apart for soft-sided scones. Bake in
   top third of oven until golden, from 10 to
   12 minutes.
Serve right away.
   Makes: 12 scones

PREPARATION: 15 MINUTES
BAKING: 12 MINUTES

BREADS

Barbecued Herb-Butter Baguette

BREADS

FRESH PARMESAN HERB LOAF

Turn your summer herb garden pickings into this flavorful bread. Wonderful warm with any salad.

Preheat oven to 350°F (180°C). Butter a 9x5-inch (2-L) loaf pan. In a bowl, whisk together

1 egg
¼ cup granulated sugar
¼ cup vegetable oil
½ tsp Worcestershire
¼ tsp hot pepper sauce

Whisk in

1 cup buttermilk

In a large bowl, stir together

2 cups all-purpose flour
3 tsp baking powder
½ tsp each baking soda and salt
¼ tsp freshly ground black pepper

Stir in

¾ cup grated Parmesan
¼ cup finely chopped fresh parsley
3 tbsp finely chopped fresh basil
½ tbsp finely chopped fresh sage
    or ¾ tsp dried leaf sage

Make a well in centre. Pour in egg mixture and stir just until combined. Turn into buttered pan. Bake in centre of preheated oven until a skewer inserted into centre comes out clean, about 50 minutes. Cool in pan 5 minutes before turning out on a rack. Store at room temperature for 3 days or cover and freeze.
Makes: 16 slices

PREPARATION: 20 MINUTES
BAKING: 50 MINUTES

MULTI-CHEESE CROUTONS

Add pizzazz to soups with these unique croutons from Baldi's Restaurant in Iroquois, Ontario.

Remove crusts from

8 slices white bread

Tear bread into very small bits or briefly whirl in a food processor until crumbs form. In a large bowl, whisk

2 eggs

Stir in fresh bread crumbs and

1 cup grated old cheddar
½ cup crumbled blue cheese
½ cup freshly grated Parmesan

until a slightly sticky dough forms. Using wet hands, shape dough on a large piece of waxed paper into a log about 1¾ inches (3 cm) in diameter and 9 inches (23 cm) long. Roll up, twist ends and refrigerate until firm, at least 1 hour or up to 3 days.

Preheat oven to 350°F (180°C). Unwrap roll, then, using a serrated knife, saw into rounds about ¼ inch (0.5 cm) thick. Place slightly apart on a lightly oiled baking sheet. Bake in centre of preheated oven for 10 minutes. Then turn and continue baking until golden and crisp, from 4 to 5 minutes.

Serve hot and crisp on soup or as nibblers with drinks or salads.
Makes: 30 rounds

PREPARATION: 15 MINUTES
REFRIGERATION: 1 HOUR
BAKING: 15 MINUTES

 MAKE AHEAD: Overwrap waxed-paper log with foil and freeze. Thaw just until they can be sliced, then bake as above.

TIPS

RISING TO THE OCCASION

Make your bread a winner with this yeast primer. Once sold only as wet or dry, yeast selection now includes fresh, traditional dry, instant, rapid-mix, bread-machine and even brewer's yeast, which can't raise a loaf of bread at all! Here's a "magic decoder" that will definitely help you rise to the occasion.

Fresh

The choice of professional bakers, fresh yeast must be refrigerated, has a storage life of a few weeks (if properly stored) and is susceptible to mold formation. But it can be frozen safely for months. It is found in the dairy case of some grocery stores in foil-wrapped cubes, or, if you own an accurate electronic scale, ask your local bakery to sell you a piece of their large block.

Traditional Active Dry Yeast

This is sold in small, flat packages (often three are joined together in a strip), vacuum-packed tins and jars, and in small packages in bulk-food stores. It can be kept for about a year in a cool dry place away from light (a refrigerator is ideal).

Quick-Rise Instant Yeast

A time-saver for when you're in a hurry, this dry yeast, also known as Rapid-Rise Instant Yeast, is stirred directly into the flour. It is activated by stirring in very warm liquids and requires only a 10-minute first rising. Then the dough is shaped for a final longer rise.

Rapid-Mix Yeast

Don't confuse this with rapid-rise instant yeast; this dry yeast is not an instant yeast. You add it directly to the flour in the recipe without dissolving it. Two full risings are then needed.

Bread-Machine Yeast

This new strain of yeast is specially formulated for bread machines. Use according to the instructions provided by the manufacturer of your bread machine, since there is a wide variance in yeast requirements, and in machine capacity and programmability.

Brewer's Yeast

Sometimes sold near bread yeasts, brewer's yeast is used as a nutritional supplement and for making beer. Don't use for making bread.

Dips, Spreads & Salsas

*Caviar raises this gorgeous LAYERED
AVOCADO DIP (see recipe page 50)
to special party status.*

DIPS, SPREADS & SALSAS

LAYERED AVOCADO DIP

This beautifully layered dip comes from Catherine Burack, owner of S'Marvelous in Toronto.

Mix together
 4 chopped hard-boiled eggs
 2 thinly sliced green onions
 ¼ tsp salt
 pinch of cayenne
Stir in
 2 tbsp mayonnaise
 2 tbsp sour cream or thick yogurt
In another bowl, mash
 2 avocados
Stir in
 1 large minced garlic clove
 2 tbsp freshly squeezed lemon juice
 ¼ tsp hot pepper sauce
In a glass bowl, about 8 inches (20 cm) wide and 2 inches (5 cm) deep, spread egg salad in an even layer. Sprinkle with
 1 cup finely chopped red onion
Spread with avocado mixture. Then thinly spread or dot with
 1¾-oz (50-g) jar red or black lumpfish or other caviar
Serve with crackers or thin slices of baguette.
 Makes: 12 to 16 servings

PREPARATION: 15 MINUTES

MAKE AHEAD: Keep finished dip refrigerated, covered, for 3 to 4 hours. Or make egg salad, chop onion and refrigerate separately for up to a day. Make avocado mixture just before serving and assemble.

LAYERED MEXICAN DIP

This is the dip to set out when the gang drops by to watch the Grey Cup or for any other special event.

Over the bottom of a deep 10-inch (25-cm) pie plate, spread
 14-oz (398-mL) can refried beans
Cover with
 1 cup light sour cream
Sprinkle with
 3.5-oz (114-mL) can sliced drained jalapeños
 14-oz (398-mL) can sliced drained pitted black olives
 1 cup diced seeded unpeeled tomatoes
 4 sliced green onions
 ½ cup grated cheddar cheese
Serve with tortilla chips for scooping.
 Makes: 8 servings

PREPARATION: 10 MINUTES

MAKE AHEAD: Refrigerate, covered, for up to 4 or 5 hours. Tomatoes may become watery as they sit.

CURRIED CHILI DIP

Curry is the surprise flavor here, and it's a welcome wake-up.

Stir together
 ½ cup chili sauce
 3 tbsp brown sugar
 1 tbsp curry powder
 1 chopped green onion
Use as a dip for sausage rolls, bread sticks or pita crisps.
 Makes: ¾ cup

PREPARATION: 5 MINUTES

MAKE AHEAD: Refrigerate, covered, until ready to serve, for up to 2 days.

Seafood Salsa Dip

This dip is an updated version of the old-fashioned tartar sauce. And it's just as fast.

Mix together
 ½ cup mild salsa
 1 tbsp horseradish
 ½ tsp lemon juice
Use as a dip for shrimp or spoon a little on steamed mussels or raw oysters.
 Makes: ½ cup

PREPARATION: 5 MINUTES

MAKE AHEAD: Refrigerate, covered, until ready to serve, for up to 2 days.

Salsa-Salmon Dip

This high-protein, low-fat dip or spread is great over thin slices of baguettes, topped with fresh dill.

Stir together
 7½-oz (213-g) can well-drained salmon
 2 tbsp salsa
 1 to 2 tbsp sour cream
 1 finely chopped green onion
Serve with pita or tortilla chips.
 Makes: ⅔ cup

PREPARATION: 5 MINUTES

MAKE AHEAD: Refrigerate, covered, until ready to serve, for up to 2 days.

Salsa-Salmon Dip

51

DIPS, SPREADS & SALSAS

CREAMY GOAT CHEESE DIP

Chèvre gives this easy dip sophistication. Surround with bread rounds or apple slices for dipping.

Stir together
   4.5-oz (140-g) roll room-temperature
      creamy goat cheese, about ½ cup
   ¾ cup light or regular sour cream
   ½ tsp coarsely ground black pepper
   ¼ tsp each sugar and salt
   pinches of chopped fresh dill, basil or
      green onions
   Makes: 1¼ cups
      PREPARATION: 5 MINUTES

MAKE AHEAD: Refrigerate, covered, until ready to serve, for up to 2 days.

BRUNCH FRUIT DIP

Whip this dip together for spreading over bagels or dipping with apples, pears or berries.

Stir together
   8-oz (250-g) container whipped
      cream cheese
   finely grated peel of 1 orange
   3 tbsp orange juice
   1 tsp granulated sugar
   ½ tsp vanilla
   Makes: 1 cup

      PREPARATION: 5 MINUTES

MAKE AHEAD: Refrigerate, covered, until ready to serve, for up to 2 days.

PIMENTO DIP

This pretty dip is very accessible. You probably have everything you need for it in your cupboard now.

In a food processor, whirl together
   4-oz (125-mL) jar drained pimentos
   ½ cup regular or light mayonnaise
   1 minced garlic clove
   ¼ tsp each salt and freshly ground
      black pepper
To make dippers, slice into ¼-inch (0.5-cm)
      thick rounds
   1 English cucumber
   Makes: 1 cup

      PREPARATION: 10 MINUTES

MAKE AHEAD: Refrigerate dip, covered, until ready to serve, for up to 2 days.

CREAMY PESTO DIP

Whether it's a casual or formal gathering, you always want to put out nibbles. This dip is perfect.

Blend together
   8 oz (250 g) whipped or spreadable light
      cream cheese
   2 tbsp pesto
Add
   pinches of salt and pepper
   ¼ to ½ tsp paprika
For dippers, consider bread sticks, vegetable
      crudités or taco chips.
   Makes: 1 cup

      PREPARATION: 5 MINUTES

MAKE AHEAD: Refrigerate, covered, until ready to serve, for up to 2 days.

GREEK BEAN SPREAD

Here's an easy dip that you can count on to impress.

In a medium-size bowl, mash just until chunky
 14-oz can drained black beans
Stir in
 1 chopped tomato
 2 minced garlic cloves
 ¼ cup finely chopped parsley
 ½ tsp salt
 ¼ tsp each dried leaf oregano, basil and
  freshly ground black pepper
Makes: 2 cups

PREPARATION: 5 MINUTES

 MAKE AHEAD: Refrigerate covered, until ready to serve, for up to 2 days. Stir before serving.

SHALLOT TARRAGON DIP

Your guests will love this very French dip.

In a frying pan over low heat, sauté
 1 tbsp vegetable oil
 1 cup finely chopped shallots
 2 minced garlic cloves
 ¼ cup white wine
Cook, stirring occasionally, until wine has
 evaporated and shallots are soft, about
 10 minutes. In a bowl, place
 1 lb (500 g) light cream cheese
Stir in warm shallots and
 ½ tsp dried leaf tarragon
 ¼ tsp each salt and black pepper
Makes: 2 cups

PREPARATION: 5 MINUTES
COOKING: 10 MINUTES

DIPS, SPREADS & SALSAS

GREEK BEAN SPREAD & SHALLOT TARRAGON DIP

SMOKED SALMON DIP & SUGAR SNAP PEAS

*Sandra Watson of Toronto uses crispy sugar snap peas for dipping into
a lemony smoked salmon dip.*

In a food processor, whirl until chopped
  ½ lb (250 g) smoked salmon
Whirl in until almost smooth
  1 cup light or regular sour cream
  1 tbsp drained capers
  1 tbsp chopped fresh dill
  1½ tsp freshly squeezed lemon juice
  dash of hot pepper sauce
Cover and refrigerate until cold, at least 1 hour
  or up to a day. In a saucepan of boiling water
  over high heat, cook for 30 seconds
  1½ lbs (750 g) trimmed sugar snap peas,
  snow peas or green beans

Drain and immediately rinse under cold
  running water. Cover and refrigerate while
  dip is chilling.
Serve dip surrounded by peas or beans
  for dipping.
Makes: 2 cups dip, about 8 servings

*PREPARATION: 15 MINUTES
COOKING: 30 SECONDS
REFRIGERATION: 1 HOUR*

MAKE AHEAD: Refrigerate covered pâté
and blanched snow peas for up to a day.
Pack for a picnic by partially filling
clear plastic cups with pâté. Then
stand snow peas upright in the pâté.

Smoked Salmon Dip & Sugar Snap Peas

SMOKED SALMON PÂTÉ

Use smoked salmon trimmings and bits instead of pricey thin slices. They work just as well here.

In a food processor, whirl until finely ground
   ½ lb (250 g) smoked salmon
Cut into cubes
   4-oz (125-g) pkg cream cheese
   ¼ cup cold unsalted butter
Add all at once to food processor. Whirl until evenly mixed. Taste and, for a more robust flavor, whirl in
   pinch of dry mustard
Whirl in
   1 tbsp chopped fresh dill
Serve with thin slices of baguette or crackers.
   Makes: 1½ cups

PREPARATION: 10 MINUTES

MAKE AHEAD: Refrigerate with plastic wrap directly on surface until ready to serve, for up to 2 days.

CHEDDAR SHERRY SPREAD

Serve this spread with pumpernickel squares or crackers. Perfect for noshing by the fireplace.

Stir together
   4-oz (125-g) pkg room-temperature light
      or regular cream cheese
   3 tbsp port or dry sherry
Stir in
   1 tbsp finely chopped green onion
   ¼ tsp caraway seeds
   pinch of black pepper
   2 cups finely grated old cheddar cheese
   Makes: 2 cups

PREPARATION: 5 MINUTES

MAKE AHEAD: Refrigerate, covered, until ready to serve, for up to 1 week.

Cheddar Sherry Spread

DIPS, SPREADS & SALSAS

SMOKED OYSTER SPREAD

This recipe is from Barbara-Jo McIntosh's book
Tin Fish Gourmet *(Raincoast Books).*

Rinse with cold water
  2 (3-oz/85-g) tins smoked oysters
Pat dry with paper towels and whirl in a food
  processor or blender with
  8-oz (250-g) pkg room-temperature
    cream cheese
  1½ tsp freshly squeezed lemon juice
  1 small minced garlic clove
  1 thinly sliced green onion
  dash of Worcestershire
Serve sprinkled with chopped fresh parsley or
  green onions accompanied by thin slices of
  French baguette or crisp crackers.
  Makes: 1½ cups

PREPARATION: 10 MINUTES

VARIATION: SMOKED TROUT SPREAD
Skin and flake 1 smoked trout into a small
bowl. Omitting smoked oysters, add remaining
ingredients. Use a fork to mash into a slightly
chunky spread.

MAKE AHEAD: Refrigerate with plastic
wrap directly on surface until ready to
serve, for up to 2 days.

BRANDIED CHICKEN LIVER PÂTÉ

*Potluck suppers in Port Union, Newfoundland, often
sport C. Milley Johnson's delightful brandied pâté.*

Wash and trim
  1 lb (500 g) chicken livers
Cut in half. In a large frying pan over medium
  heat, melt
  ⅓ cup butter
Stir in
  1 small finely chopped onion
  2 minced garlic cloves
Cook, stirring occasionally until onion has
  softened, about 5 minutes. Add chicken
  livers and
  ¼ cup brandy
  ½ tsp salt
  ¼ tsp each crushed dried rosemary, freshly
    ground black pepper and grated nutmeg
Cook, stirring often, until livers are brown on
  outside but still pink inside, about another
  3 minutes. Then purée in food processor or
  blender. Taste and stir in
  1 tsp coarsely cracked black pepper
    (optional)
Pour into a small bowl, press plastic wrap into
  surface and refrigerate until firm, for at least
  2 hours or up to 2 days. Serve in the bowl or
  turn out. Sprinkle with
  chopped parsley
Serve with crisp crackers.
  Makes: 2½ cups

PREPARATION: 15 MINUTES
COOKING: 8 MINUTES
REFRIGERATION: 2 HOURS

MAKE AHEAD: Refrigerate with plastic
wrap pressed directly on surface until
ready to serve, for up to 2 days.

ROASTED RED PEPPER-CHÈVRE SPREAD

Here's a chic spread for baguette slices. Top with baby shrimp, a fan of snow peas or tiny fresh basil leaves. Also great in tortilla rolls.

Preheat oven to 400°F (200°C).
  Slice in half, core and seed
  1 large red pepper
Place cut-side down on a foil-lined baking sheet. Roast, uncovered, until part of skin is blackened, from 20 to 25 minutes. When cool enough to handle, peel off skin.
(Or use ½ cup drained bottled roasted red pepper.)
In a blender or food processor, whirl roasted red pepper with
  4-oz (125-g) roll herbed chèvre or creamy goat cheese, about ½ cup

Scrape into a small bowl and stir in
  2 thinly sliced green onions
Cover and refrigerate until thickened, for at least 2 hours or up to 2 days. Spread over tortillas, top with spinach and basil, roll up and slice.
Makes: ¾ cup

> PREPARATION: 5 MINUTES
> BROILING: 25 MINUTES
> REFRIGERATION: 2 HOURS

MAKE AHEAD: Refrigerate, covered, until ready to serve, for up to 2 days.

ROASTED RED PEPPER-CHÈVRE SPREAD

RED PEPPER & BLACK BEAN SALSA

*This two-way salsa is a smart addition
to a buffet spread.*

In a large bowl, stir together
    19-oz (540-mL) can drained black beans
    1 coarsely chopped seeded red pepper
    1 chopped yellow or green zucchini
    ½ chopped red onion
In another bowl, whisk
    3 tbsp olive oil
    2 tbsp freshly squeezed lime juice
    generous pinches of salt, freshly ground
        black pepper and cayenne
Stir into vegetables with
    ¼ cup chopped fresh coriander
Taste and add more salt and pepper if needed.
    Refrigerate until cold, about 1 hour or
    preferably overnight.
Makes: 4 cups

PREPARATION: 15 MINUTES
REFRIGERATION: 1 HOUR

MAKE AHEAD: Refrigerate, covered,
until ready to serve, for up to 3 days.

HOT PEPPER & CORIANDER SALSA

*A spoonful of this colorful salsa brings alive
grilled halibut, swordfish or sea bass.*

Seed and cut into thin julienne strips or
    finely chop
    2 large hot banana peppers
        or 6 seeded jalapeños
Combine in a bowl with
    4 to 5 chopped seeded large tomatoes
Stir into pepper mixture until coated
    2 tbsp olive oil
    1 tbsp white vinegar
    ¼ tsp each salt and freshly ground
        black pepper
Then stir in
    ½ cup chopped fresh coriander
Serve right away or leave at room temperature
    for 3 to 4 hours to give flavors a chance
    to mingle.
Makes: 2 cups

PREPARATION: 15 MINUTES

*Hot Pepper &
Coriander Salsa*

Mango & Sweet Pepper Salsa

*This gorgeous combo is a great dress-up
for grilled sea bass or halibut.*

Preheat broiler. Cut in half and seed
   3 red peppers
   2 jalapeños
Broil on a baking sheet, turning once, until
   just slightly singed on edges, from 15 to
   20 minutes. In a bowl, stir together
   3 tbsp freshly squeezed lemon juice
   3 tbsp olive oil
   1 minced garlic clove
   ¼ tsp each salt and pepper
Peel and chop
   1 ripe mango
Stir mango along with any mango juices into
   lemon mixture. Without peeling, coarsely
   chop broiled sweet peppers and finely chop
   jalapeños. Stir into mango mixture with
   ¼ cup chopped fresh coriander
      or Italian parsley
Toss until well mixed.
   Makes: 2 cups

   PREPARATION: 10 MINUTES
   BROILING: 20 MINUTES

MAKE AHEAD: Refrigerate, covered,
until ready to use, for up to 2 days. For
best flavor, serve at room temperature.

Spicy Cucumber Salsa

*Make this salsa when you're having a party. It's a
great low-cal way to dress up grilled chicken or fish.*

In a large bowl, stir together
   1 chopped seeded English cucumber
   ½ chopped small red onion
   1 chopped seeded small red pepper
   1 grated carrot (optional)
In another bowl, whisk together
   2 tbsp vegetable oil
   3 tbsp rice wine vinegar
      or 2 tbsp white vinegar
   1 tsp granulated sugar (optional)
   ¼ to ½ tsp hot red pepper flakes
   pinches of salt and freshly ground
      black pepper
Stir into vegetables with
   ½ cup chopped fresh coriander
Cover and refrigerate for at least 2 hours or
   up to 1 day.
   Makes: 4 cups

   PREPARATION: 15 MINUTES
   REFRIGERATION: 2 HOURS

MAKE AHEAD: Refrigerate, covered,
until ready to serve, for up to 1 day.

DIPS, SPREADS & SALSAS

MEDITERRANEAN CRANBERRY SPREAD

*Feta and dried cranberries produce
a remarkably refreshing mix.*

In a blender or food processor, whirl until fairly
    smooth
    1 cup crumbled feta cheese
    2 tbsp olive oil
Add
    ¼ cup dried cranberries
Whirl until finely chopped. Taste and whirl in
    pinches of dried rosemary and ground
        white or black pepper
Cover and refrigerate until thickened, at least
    2 hours or up to 2 days. Serve spread on thin
    slices of whole-grain bread topped with a
    sprig of rosemary. Or spread over tortillas,
    top with slices of arugula or spinach, roll up
    and slice.
Makes: 1 cup

PREPARATION: 10 MINUTES
REFRIGERATION: 2 HOURS

MAKE AHEAD: Refrigerate, covered,
until ready to serve, for up to 2 days.

CHEESE & CHUTNEY SPREAD

*Make this intriguing spread in 5 minutes to use over
crackers or for dipping with celery or Belgian endive.*

Stir together
    8-oz (250-g) container whipped
        cream cheese
    3 to 4 tbsp mango chutney
    ½ tsp curry powder
    ¼ tsp ground ginger
Makes: 1 cup

PREPARATION: 5 MINUTES

CHÈVRE SPREAD

*The distinctive taste of chèvre works beautifully
with the assertive flavor of sun-dried tomatoes.*

With a fork, mash together until blended
    4.5-oz (140-g) roll creamy goat cheese
    ¼ cup sour cream
Stir in
    1 very finely chopped green onion
    2 very finely chopped oil-packed sun-dried
        tomatoes or sun-dried tomatoes soaked
        in hot water until pliable
Pack into a pretty dish. Use right away or cover
    and refrigerate up to 3 days. Great as a spread
    on crackers. Or spread over tortillas, add a
    few spinach or coriander leaves, roll up and
    slice into appetizers.
Makes: 1 cup

PREPARATION: 15 MINUTES

BRUNCH BRIE

*Serve this elegant warm Brie surrounded by apple
and pear wedges or vegetable sticks for dipping.*

Preheat oven to 400°F (200°C). Remove rind
    from
    1 whole round of Brie
Place cheese in a 10-inch (24-cm) quiche pan or
    pie plate that it fits comfortably in. Bake in
    preheated oven just until cheese melts and
    fills pan, about 10 minutes. Sprinkle with
    chopped cooked bacon
    finely chopped red and green peppers
    fresh coriander or parsley
Makes: 10 servings

PREPARATION: 5 MINUTES
COOKING: 10 MINUTES

TIPS

SPREAD IT AROUND
Here's how to make the fillings in this section look as good as they taste.

New Rolls
Thinly spread filling over flour tortillas. Or remove crusts from sandwich bread slices, then flatten with a rolling pin before spreading. Roll up tightly, cover with plastic wrap and twist ends closed. Refrigerate at least 1 hour or up to 1 day. When ready to serve, slice into ½-inch (1-cm) rounds.

Dainty Cutouts
Remove crusts from bread slices. Spread slices with filling. Cut into squares, triangles or rounds using a cookie cutter. Decorate with fresh herbs such as dill, basil leaves and chives, or with thin slices of gherkins, a sprinkling of chopped fresh parsley or diced colorful peppers or carrots. Loosely cover with plastic wrap, then a dampened paper towel. Refrigerate until ready to serve.

The Whole Loaf
Ask your baker to horizontally slice a sandwich loaf (a square flat-topped loaf) lengthwise into 3 or 4 slices. Remove crusts. Reserving one plain slice for the top, spread remaining with different fillings about ½ inch (0.5 cm) thick. Stack coated slices. Top with plain slice. Ice outside with whipped cream cheese. Refrigerate at least 1 hour or overnight. For a holiday motif, decorate with fresh parsley leaves and cranberries. Slice like a loaf cake.

LOW-FAT DIPPER SUGGESTIONS
- huge soft pretzels or hard pretzel sticks
- whole-wheat pitas or focaccia warmed on the barbecue or in the oven, then cut into wedges
- an assortment of sweet red, yellow, orange, purple or green peppers, seeded and cut into fat triangles
- sections of fruit such as clementines, red and green apples, pears and mango
- barbecued chicken fingers

DIPS, SPREADS & SALSAS

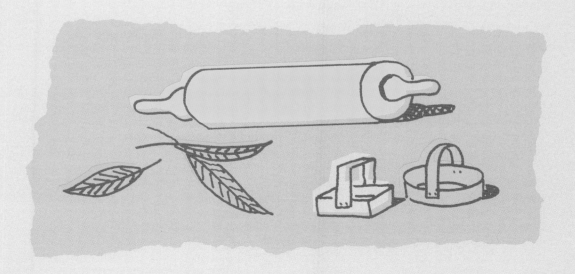

DRINKS

This icy cold TERRIFIC MARGARITA (see recipe page 64) epitomizes the best of hot weather sipping.

DRINKS

TERRIFIC MARGARITAS

This classic cooler is perfect for a hot day poolside party or barbecue.

Moisten rims of two cocktail glasses with
    1 lime wedge
Dip rims in
    salt
In a cocktail shaker, combine
    3 tbsp tequila
    3 tbsp triple sec or orange liqueur
    2 tbsp freshly squeezed lime juice
    a little crushed ice
Shake until frothy, then pour into glasses.
    Add more crushed ice and garnish each
    with a lime wedge propped on the rim.
    Makes: 2 drinks

PREPARATION: 10 MINUTES

APPLE ICED TEA

Everyone loves iced tea. It's the perfect refresher course on a hot day.

Steep for 5 minutes
    4 tea bags
in
    2 cups boiling water
Remove bags. Add
    48-oz (1.36-L) can unsweetened apple juice
Chill. Serve over ice.
    Makes: 8 cups

PREPARATION: 5 MINUTES

STRAWBERRY-PINEAPPLE COLADA

This frothy concoction will make a big splash at your next pool party.

In a blender or food processor, whirl
    until smooth
    2 cups unsweetened pineapple juice
    1 cup unsweetened coconut milk
    1 pint (500 mL) hulled strawberries, about
      2 cups, or 10-oz (300-g) pkg frozen
      unsweetened strawberries
    1/2 cup rum
Pour over ice in tall glasses. Garnish with
    a fresh strawberry and sprinkle with
    toasted coconut.
    Makes: 4½ cups or 6 to 8 servings

PREPARATION: 10 MINUTES

MULLED CRANBERRY ROSÉ

Here's a pleasant sipper that also gives an enticing aroma throughout the house.

In a large saucepan over high heat, bring to a boil
    1 cup water
    1/2 cup granulated sugar
    5 cloves
    2 cinnamon sticks
Reduce heat to low and simmer, uncovered, for
    5 minutes. Remove from heat and stir in
    40-oz (1.14-L) bottle cranberry juice
    24-oz (750-mL) bottle rosé or blush wine
    1/2 cup freshly squeezed lemon juice
Heat until steaming and serve hot. Or for a cold
    punch, cover and refrigerate.
    Makes: 8 cups or 13 (5-oz/150-mL)
    punch glasses

PREPARATION: 10 MINUTES
COOKING: 5 MINUTES

MERRY MULLED CIDER

Serve mugs of this fragrant drink in front of the fireplace after a day on the slopes.

In a large saucepan, heat
  8 cups apple cider
  2 (1-inch/2.5-cm) cinnamon sticks
  5 whole allspice
Heat until cider just starts to bubble around the edges. Lower heat, cover and simmer for about 10 minutes to develop flavor. Add
  ½ cup brandy (optional)
Serve with a pat of cold butter floating on top of each mug.
  Makes: 8½ cups

  PREPARATION: 10 MINUTES

TROPICAL SHAKE

Whip up this passion-fruit drink whenever you want a taste of the Caribbean.

In a blender or food processor, whirl until blended
  ½ cup mango or apricot nectar
  ⅓ cup unsweetened coconut milk
  ¼ cup orange juice
  ¼ cup rum (optional)
  5 ice cubes
Pour into tall or prettily-shaped glasses and garnish with a slice of lime.
  Makes: 1⅓ cups or 2 servings

  PREPARATION: 5 MINUTES

TROPICAL SHAKE

DRINKS

TREE-TRIMMING PUNCH

*This pretty punch will keep everyone
happy until the tree is all lit up.*

Wash and dry thoroughly
  2 bunches seedless grapes, preferably green
    and deep red
Freeze in bunches on a baking sheet. Meanwhile,
  in a large punch bowl, stir together
  40-oz (1.14-L) bottle cranberry juice
  12-oz (355-mL) can frozen fruit punch
    concentrate
  12-oz (355-mL) can frozen orange juice
    concentrate
  6 juice cans cold water
Stir in
  1½ cups (375 mL) rum or 12-oz (355-mL)
    can ginger ale (optional)
Taste and add more rum or ginger ale.
  Refrigerate until chilled. To serve, pluck
  frozen grapes from stems and float in punch
  like ice cubes.
Makes: 18 cups or 36 servings

PREPARATION: 15 MINUTES
FREEZING: 30 MINUTES

GRAND BRANDIED EGGNOG

*Reserve this luxurious number for
your Christmas open house.*

In a large bowl, stir together
  1 quart (1 L) eggnog
  finely grated peel of 1 small orange
  ¼ cup Grand Marnier or other
    orange liqueur
  ¼ cup brandy
Makes: 4½ cups

PREPARATION: 5 MINUTES

WARM SPICED EGGNOG

*Serve up this holiday warmer with
a cinnamon stirrer stick.*

In a large saucepan over low heat, heat
  1 quart (1 L) eggnog
  1 cinnamon stick
  ¼ tsp cardamom
  generous pinch of ground nutmeg
Heat just until warm. Do not boil.
Serve warm or cold.
Makes: 4 cups

PREPARATION: 5 MINUTES

WASSAIL

*A steaming glass of red wine punch is a great
accompaniment to a roaring fire on Christmas Day.*

In a large saucepan over medium-high heat,
  stirring often, warm
  24-oz (750-mL) bottle dry red wine
    such as cabernet sauvignon
    or dry rosé such as cabernet franc
  2 cups pineapple juice
  2 cups apple juice
  ½ cup brown sugar
  2 cinnamon sticks
  ¼ tsp ground cardamom
  ¼ tsp ground cloves
Heat until sugar dissolves and mixture begins
  to bubble. Reduce heat to low and simmer,
  uncovered, for 20 minutes to develop flavors.
Top each glass with
  1 thin slice of lemon
*Makes: 6 cups, about 10
(5-oz/150-mL) servings*

PREPARATION: 10 MINUTES
COOKING: 20 MINUTES

CHIC CHAMPAGNE PUNCH

Honey and apricot nectar plus orange liqueur raises inexpensive champagne to black-tie status.

In a large punch bowl, stir together
 ¼ cup liquid honey
 ¼ cup apricot nectar
Just before serving, pour down sides of bowl
 and gently stir
 24-oz (750-mL) bottle cold champagne
 or sparkling wine
Add ice cubes. Taste and stir in
 ¼ cup orange liqueur (optional)
Serve right away.
 Makes: 4 cups or 6 (5-oz/150-mL)
 punch glasses

 PREPARATION: 10 MINUTES

SHERRIED CRANBERRY PUNCH

A bottle of sherry goes a long way in this festive punch.

In a large pitcher, combine
 40-oz (1.14-L) bottle cranberry juice
 1 thinly sliced orange
 1 thinly sliced lime
 1 cup fresh cranberries (optional)
Cover and refrigerate, stirring occasionally,
 for several hours or overnight. Just before
 serving, add
 24-oz (750-mL) bottle chilled
 medium-dry sherry
 Makes: 16 (½-cup) servings

 PREPARATION: 10 MINUTES

SHERRIED CRANBERRY PUNCH

NEGRONI

Italy's legendary aperitif, the bitter bright-red Campari, is a staple in this classic drink.

Mix together
   2 tbsp (1 oz) gin
   1 tbsp (½ oz) Campari
   1 tbsp (½ oz) sweet red vermouth
Pour over ice cubes. Top up with
   soda water (optional)
Garnish with an orange wheel.
   Makes: 1 drink

PREPARATION: 5 MINUTES

CITRUS BEER BLASTER

Add a lemony twist to your favorite beer with this refreshing sip.

Into a beer glass, spoon
   2 tbsp frozen limeade or
     lemonade concentrate
Slowly pour down side of glass
   12-oz (341-mL) bottle of beer or ale
Gently stir. Squeeze over top
   wedge of lime or lemon
Drop into glass.
   Makes: 1 drink

PREPARATION: 5 MINUTES

CLASSIC MARTINI

Greet your guests with martinis. The classic martini is made with gin, but vodka is good too.

Into a shaker, pour (see Tips, opposite, for
   a perfect martini)
   ¼ cup (2 oz) gin
Splash with
   1½ tsp (¼ oz) or less dry white vermouth
Add
   dash of orange bitters or twist a long strip
     of orange rind
   into the shaker.
Shake, then strain into a martini glass. Garnish
   with a twist of lemon peel.
   Makes: 1 martini

PREPARATION: 5 MINUTES

VARIATION: Agent 007 popularized martinis made with Russian vodka. To make a Classic 007, pour ¼ cup (2 oz) vodka into a shaker and add a splash of dry vermouth. Shake, then strain and garnish with olives.

Classic Martini

DRINKS

ROB ROY

Named for a Scottish outlaw, this drink is good served either straight up or on the rocks.

Shake over ice cubes
   3 tbsp (1 ½ oz) scotch whiskey
   1 tbsp (½ oz) sweet red vermouth
   dash of Angostura bitters
Serve garnished with a cherry or olives.
   Makes: 1 drink

PREPARATION: 5 MINUTES

RUSTY NAIL

Scotch lovers double their pleasure in this classic sipper, since Drambuie is a scotch-based liqueur.

Pour into a cocktail glass without ice
   3 tbsp (1 ½ oz) scotch whiskey
Float on top or layer in an old-fashioned glass
   with ice cubes
   1 tbsp (1 oz) Drambuie
Don't stir.
   Makes: 1 drink

PREPARATION: 5 MINUTES

TIPS

Perfect Martini
To make a martini, remember James Bond's famed preference – shaken, not stirred. Add ice cubes to a shaker until two-thirds full and pour in the liquid ingredients. Give it a few fast shakes, then strain it into a martini glass. If you don't have a standard bar shaker, use a container with a tight-fitting lid or fit a smaller rimmed container into a large one so that it seals temporarily. The liquids should be in contact with the ice just long enough to chill the martini, but not melt the ice. For a frosted effect, place glasses and gin in the freezer before creating the martinis.

Popping the Bubbly
To safely and smartly open sparkling wine or champagne, thoroughly chill the bottle. Gently remove foil and wire cork holder. Drape a tea towel over the bottle and grasp the cork through the towel. With your other hand under the towel, twist the bottle, not the cork. The cork should slip slowly and easily out of the bottle. Pour immediately and enjoy, since sparkling wines loose their fizz quickly.

FESTIVE

*In SPLENDID PUFF PASTRY STARS
(see recipe page 72), appetizers take a starring
role with six different holiday toppings.*

SPLENDID PUFF PASTRY STARS

*To see you through the festive season, bake up a big batch
of these stars with six different toppings.*

Preheat oven to 400°F (200°C). Cut into 2 pieces
14-oz (379-g) pkg frozen puff pastry, defrosted
On a lightly floured surface, roll each piece into
a 9x18-inch (23x46-cm) rectangle. Using a
2½-inch (6-cm) star-shaped cookie cutter,
cut out stars and lay slightly apart on a
foil-lined baking sheet. Spread with a topping
(see below). Then bake in preheated oven
until golden, from 10 to 12 minutes. Repeat,
gathering any scraps into a ball, rolling out
and cutting more stars.
Makes: 80 stars

PREPARATION: 20 MINUTES
BAKING: 12 MINUTES

HOT PEPPER JELLY & CHEESE
Thinly spread creamy goat or cream cheese
over stars. Spoon ¼ tsp hot pepper jelly
in centre. Sprinkle with chopped fresh basil.

MUSTARD & OLIVE
Lightly brush Dijon on stars. Sprinkle with
grated Fontina or provolone cheese. Lay a thick
slice of pimento-stuffed green olives in centres.

CRANBERRY
Thinly spread cranberry sauce on stars and
sprinkle with grated orange peel.

MEXICAN PIZZA
Lightly spread stars with a thick hot salsa. Scatter
with diced thin slices of pepperoni. Sprinkle
with grated mozzarella or Monterey Jack.

CHUTNEY & CHEDDAR
Thinly spread chutney on stars. Sprinkle
with grated cheddar, then sprinkle with
sliced green onions.

CAESAR TOPPING
Thinly spread stars with creamy Caesar
dressing. Sprinkle with freshly ground black
pepper, cooked bacon bits and grated
Parmesan.

 MAKE AHEAD: Prepared stars can be
frozen before or after baking. Freeze
unbaked stars on baking sheets until
firm, about 2 hours. Layer stars in an
airtight container between sheets of waxed
paper. Bake frozen stars on baking sheets at
400°F (200°C) for 12 to 14 minutes. Or freeze
baked stars, then reheat frozen on baking sheet
in 350°F (180°C) oven for 10 minutes.

FESTIVE WARM BRIE

*A festive combination of red-and-green toppings give holiday pizzazz to
a warm Brie – and it can be readied well ahead of party time.*

Preheat oven to 350°F (180°C). Leaving sides and bottom intact, thinly slice top rind off 4-inch (10-cm) wide Brie or Camembert

Stir topping together (see right) and spoon over cheese. To heat in oven, place on a foil-lined baking sheet and bake, uncovered, in preheated oven until warm, from 8 to 10 minutes. Or place on a plate, loosely cover with waxed paper and microwave on medium until warm, from 1½ to 2 minutes. Serve right away with water crackers.
Makes: 4 to 6 servings per round

PREPARATION: 10 MINUTES
BAKING: 10 MINUTES

JALAPEÑO PEPPER TOPPING
Stir ¼ cup finely chopped red pepper with I finely chopped seeded jalapeño or I tbsp chopped canned green chilies and I small minced garlic clove or ½ tsp bottled minced garlic.

TOMATO BRUSCHETTA TOPPING
Stir ¼ cup seeded finely chopped ripe tomato with I small minced garlic clove or ½ tsp bottled minced garlic, ½ tsp olive oil, ¼ tsp dried basil and pinch of ground black pepper.

MAKE AHEAD: Completely prepare cheese and refrigerate for up to a day. Then bake.

FESTIVE WARM BRIE

FESTIVE

FESTIVE

Light 'n' Festive Tourtière Tartlets

Serve lightly spiced tourtière as attractive bite-size appetizers that can be made ahead.

Preheat oven to 425°F (220°C). Arrange on a baking sheet
    16 homemade or 21 store-bought frozen small tart shells
In a large frying pan over medium heat, melt
    2 tsp butter
Add
    1 finely chopped onion
    1 lb (500 g) ground turkey, chicken or veal
    ½ tsp each salt and dried leaf thyme
    ¼ tsp each ground cloves, cinnamon, rubbed sage and black pepper
Cook, stirring often with a fork to keep meat separated until it loses its pink color, about 15 minutes. Whisk together
    1 egg
    ¾ cup sour cream
Remove meat mixture from heat and stir in sour cream mixture and
    ¼ cup finely chopped Italian parsley
Heap mixture in tart shells. Place on lowest rack of oven and bake in preheated oven, 8 minutes. Reduce heat to 350°F (180°C) and continue baking until filling is set, about 14 more minutes. Serve hot.
Makes: 21 small tarts

PREPARATION: 10 MINUTES
COOKING: 15 MINUTES
BAKING: 22 MINUTES

 MAKE AHEAD: Bake tarts, cool and refrigerate or freeze. Reheat, uncovered, on a baking sheet in a 350°F (180°C) oven. Cold tarts need from 10 to 12 minutes and frozen from 15 to 18 minutes.

Cranberry BBQ Chicken Wings

Here's a clever spirited way to dress up chicken wings for your Christmas party.

In a large bowl, whisk together
    ½ cup jellied cranberry sauce
    ½ cup barbecue sauce
    ¼ cup vegetable oil
Stir in
    4 lbs (2 kg) small chicken wings
Cover and refrigerate for at least 1 hour or up to a day. Stir occasionally. Preheat oven to 400°F (200°C). Place wings slightly apart on greased wire racks set over foil-lined baking sheets. Basting occasionally for first 15 minutes, bake in centre of preheated oven, turning once, until nicely browned, from 30 to 35 minutes.
Serve hot with sour cream or blue cheese dressing for dipping.
Makes: 12 appetizer servings

PREPARATION: 10 MINUTES
REFRIGERATION: 1 HOUR
BAKING: 35 MINUTES

Jolly Mincemeat Meatballs

In 10 minutes or less turn a package of frozen store-bought meatballs into a festive appetizer.

In a large saucepan, heat
    1 cup mincemeat
    ¾ cup hot or medium salsa
    ⅓ cup water
Add
    ½ (2-lb/907-g) pkg frozen Swedish meatballs
Cover and stir often over medium heat until hot, from 10 to 13 minutes. Keep hot in a chafing dish. Serve with toothpicks.
Makes: 32 meatballs

PREPARATION: 10 MINUTES
COOKING: 13 MINUTES

FESTIVE

CHRISTMAS PIZZAS

These festive pizzas, shaped into stars, bells, Christmas trees and gingerbread people, are an original addition to any Christmas gathering, especially for kids.

Preheat oven to 425°F (220°C). Lightly grease baking sheets. Using scissors or cookie cutters, cut out festive shapes such as Christmas trees, stars and bells, or use a large cookie cutter to create gingerbread people from
12 store-bought small pizza crusts, each about 6 inches (15 cm) wide, or 3 large pizza crusts

Arrange cutouts on sheet. Spread with
2 cups pizza or spaghetti sauce

Sprinkle with
½ cup thinly sliced pitted black olives
2 diced sweet peppers, one red and one green

Cover with
2 cups grated cheese, such as mozzarella or Fontina

Bake on bottom rack of preheated oven until golden and bubbling, about 10 minutes. Serve immediately.

Makes: 12 servings

PREPARATION: 20 MINUTES
BAKING: 10 MINUTES

MAKE AHEAD: Prepare pizzas on baking sheets and leave at room temperature up to an hour before baking, or refrigerate, loosely covered, for up to a day.

CHRISTMAS PIZZAS & CRANBERRY BBQ CHICKEN WINGS

FESTIVE

SPIRIT OF CHRISTMAS PÂTÉ

This holiday pâté comes from Mimi's Ocean Grill in Mahone Bay.
Mimi adds deep-red dried cranberries for that sweet-tart taste.

In a large saucepan, cover and bring to a boil
   6 cups water
   1 quartered onion
   3 large whole garlic cloves
   2 bay leaves
   1 tsp salt
Reduce heat to low. Simmer, 10 minutes. Add
   1 lb (500 g) trimmed chicken livers
Cover and barely simmer, 5 minutes. Don't
   overcook. Drain, discarding liquid and bay
   leaves. Then whirl remainder in a food
   processor until almost smooth. Add
   4-oz (125-g) pkg cream cheese,
     cut into cubes
   1 tsp Dijon
   ½ tsp each dried leaf thyme, ground nutmeg
     and freshly ground black pepper
   ¼ tsp ground cloves or allspice

Whirl until smooth. Turn into a bowl. Stir in
   ½ to ¾ cup coarsely chopped dried
     cranberries
For extra color, stir in some finely chopped fresh
   parsley. Place plastic wrap directly on surface
   and refrigerate until thickened, about 4 hours
   or up to 2 days. Decorate with sprigs of fresh
   parsley and several cranberries. Serve chilled
   with toast wedges or crisp crackers.
Makes: 2 cups, for 10 to 12 servings

PREPARATION: 30 MINUTES
COOKING: 15 MINUTES
REFRIGERATION: 4 HOURS

MAKE AHEAD: Prepare pâté and
refrigerate for up to 2 days.

Spirit of Christmas Pâté

CHRISTMAS CHEDDAR CANES

Candy cane-shaped cheese sticks are the only nibbles you'll need with drinks before a holiday dinner party.

Preheat oven to 400°F (200°C). Cut into 2 pieces
14-oz (379-g) pkg frozen puff pastry, defrosted

Cover one piece and roll out the other piece on a floured board until a thin 9x18-inch (23x46-cm) rectangle. Spread over half of this piece
1 cup finely grated old cheddar

Sprinkle with
¼ tsp cayenne
2 tbsp finely chopped parsley

Fold over uncoated half to cover filling. Roll out again to form a 9x18-inch (23x46-cm) rectangle. Cut dough into strips about ¾ inch (2 cm) wide and 9 inches (23 cm) long. Gently twist each strip, then place on a baking sheet forming a candy-cane shape with an exaggerated hook, since canes shrink during baking.

Bake in preheated oven until puffed and golden, from 8 to 10 minutes. Meanwhile repeat process with remaining pastry using another
1 cup grated cheddar
¼ tsp cayenne
2 tbsp finely chopped parsley

Carefully remove warm canes to a rack to cool.
Makes: 48 canes

PREPARATION: 20 MINUTES
BAKING: 10 MINUTES

MAKE AHEAD: Store baked, cooled canes in an airtight container in the refrigerator for up to a month or freeze.

Christmas
Cheddar Canes

FESTIVE

FESTIVE DEVILED EGGS

Red peppers and pesto create a Christmas look in these easy-to-make deviled eggs.

Slice lengthwise
    8 hard-boiled eggs, peeled
Remove yolks and mash with
    ¼ cup mayonnaise
Divide in half and stir into one half
    3 to 4 tsp hot red pepper relish or ¼ cup
       finely chopped roasted red pepper
       or pimentos
    1 to 2 tbsp finely chopped dill pickle
    pinch of dillweed
Into other half, stir
    4 to 6 tsp pesto
Fill hollows of eggs, half and half, with some of
    each. Decorate with sprigs of fresh parsley
    or slivers of red pepper or dill pickle. If not
    serving right away, loosely cover with plastic
    and refrigerate for up to a day.
Makes: 16 halves

PREPARATION: 20 MINUTES

MAKE AHEAD: Prepare eggs. Cover and refrigerate for up to a day.

HOLIDAY CHEDDAR TARTLETS

Nippy cheddar and spicy salsa add up to great taste in these incredibly easy-to-do Southwestern tarts.

Preheat oven to 375°F (190°C). Stir together
    ½ cup grated cheddar
    2 tbsp salsa
Spoon about a tablespoon into
    10 mini store-bought frozen tart shells
Top with
    slice of pimento-stuffed green olive
Place tarts on a baking sheet. Bake on bottom
    rack of preheated oven until bubbling,
    about 12 minutes. Let sit for 10 minutes.
Makes: 10 mini tartlets

PREPARATION: 10 MINUTES
BAKING: 12 MINUTES

CHEDDAR-CRANBERRY SPREAD

Dried cranberries add pizzazz to this easy cheddar spread. Serve surrounded by slices of bread.

Stir together
    8-oz (250-g) pkg whipped or spreadable
       cream cheese
    2 tbsp milk
    ¼ tsp each dry mustard and cayenne
Stir in
    2 cups grated old cheddar cheese
    2 tbsp very finely chopped dried cranberries
       or toasted nuts
Serve with tiny pretzels or thin slices of
    multigrain baguette.
Makes: 1 cup

PREPARATION: 5 MINUTES

MAKE AHEAD: Refrigerate, covered, until ready to serve, for up to 3 days.

NEW SAUSAGE ROLLS

*Italian sausage gives a taste boost and puff pastry slashes the
prep time in these holiday classics.*

Preheat oven to 400°F (200°C). Cut into 3 pieces
14-oz (397-g) pkg frozen puff pastry, defrosted
On a lightly floured surface, roll 1 piece to a
6x12-inch (15x30-cm) rectangle. Cut in
half lengthwise
3 cooked Italian sausage
Lay 2 halves, end to end, curved sides down, on
pastry, close to long edge. Roll snugly. Trim
off any excess dough and tuck pastry ends
under flat side of sausage. Pinch to seal. Slice
into 1-inch (2.5-cm) lengths. Repeat with
remaining sausages and pastry.

Place seam-side down on a baking sheet,
1 inch (2.5 cm) apart. Bake in preheated
oven until golden, about 25 minutes.
Makes: 36 rolls

PREPARATION: 20 MINUTES
BAKING: 25 MINUTES

MAKE AHEAD: Prepare rolls and place
on a baking sheet. Cover loosely with
greased waxed paper, then a damp
towel. Refrigerate for up to half a day
before baking. Or bake rolls and refrigerate up to
2 days or freeze. Reheat in a 350°F (180°C) oven.

NEW SAUSAGE ROLLS & HOLIDAY CHEDDAR TARTLETS

FESTIVE

TOURTIÈRE MEATBALLS

With parsley-orange zest coating and Dijon dipping sauce, these herbed meatballs seem elegantly exotic, but the ingredients are truly down-home. Wonderful made with ground beef, chicken, veal or turkey.

Preheat oven to 350°F (180°C). In a large oiled
  frying pan over medium heat, sauté
  1 finely chopped onion
  1 finely chopped celery stalk
  until onion is soft, about 5 minutes. In a large
  bowl, stir together until well mixed
  1 beaten egg
  2 tbsp water
  2 slices fresh bread, made into crumbs, or
    ¼ cup store-bought fine dry bread crumbs
  ½ tsp each dried leaf thyme and salt
  ¼ tsp each ground cloves, cinnamon, dried
    leaf sage and black pepper
Work in onion mixture and
  1 lb (500 g) ground beef, veal or poultry
Roll into ¾-inch (2-cm) balls. Place slightly
  apart on a greased baking sheet with shallow
  sides. Bake in centre of preheated oven,
  uncovered and stirring occasionally, until
  browned, about 20 minutes.

Immediately toss meatballs, while warm, in
  a mixture of
  ¼ cup finely chopped parsley
  1 large minced garlic clove
  finely grated peel of 1 orange
For a dipping sauce, stir together
  ½ cup light mayonnaise
  1 to 2 tbsp Dijon
Makes: 30 meatballs

PREPARATION: 30 MINUTES
COOKING: 5 MINUTES
BAKING: 20 MINUTES

MAKE AHEAD: Covered and refrigerated
separately, plain baked meatballs and
sauce will keep refrigerated for 2 days.
  Or freeze meatballs up to 2 months.
Reheat, stirring often, covered, in microwave
on high for 4 minutes or uncovered, in 350°F
(180°C) oven for 8 to 10 minutes. Immediately
toss hot meatballs in parsley-orange mixture.

Tourtière Meatballs

TIPS

On-the-Spot Merry Nibbles

Need an appetizer fast? A quick trip to the store and you'll have all the fixings for these canapés:

- Core and slice unpeeled apples into ¼-inch (0.5-cm) slices. Top with a small piece of Cambozola, Gorgonzola or Brie. Finish with a toasted walnut or pecan half.

- Core and slice an unpeeled pear into ¼-inch (0.5-cm) slices. Top with a wedge of pâté. Add a dab of thick cranberry or lingonberry sauce.

- Fill hollowed-out cherry tomatoes with smoked salmon mixed with egg salad or a seafood pâté. Top with fresh dill or red caviar.

- Separate Belgium endive into leaves. Spoon creamy goat cheese or a flavored cream cheese into centres. Top with chopped green onion or basil.

Festive Beverages

For a variety of festive beverages, see Drinks, page 62.

Healthier Holidays

When dinner is finger food at a holiday party, balance the often fat-laden snacks with refreshing fruit and vegetables served with a smart good-for-you dip.

- Slices of melon, apple and pear or clementine sections are delicious dipped into thick drained yogurt stirred with a little grated orange peel and honey to taste. To preserve their pristine white flesh, cut slices of apple and pear close to serving time, then dip in diluted lemon juice.

- Surround a bowl of tzatziki, a thickened yogurt sauce, with single-bite pieces of carrot, celery, broccoli, red pepper and cauliflower. Small pieces of sturdy vegetables are both neater to nosh and discourage "double dipping." Crisp baked tortilla chips, pretzels and tiny rice cakes for dipping are crunchy, almost fat-free and a good way to add grains.

NIBBLES

*PEPPERY CHEESE CRISPS (see recipe page 84)
are whirled together in a food processor
in a snap, then baked like cookies.*

NIBBLES

PEPPERY CHEESE CRISPS

*Here's the perfect answer to what to have
on hand to serve with drinks.*

Preheat oven to 350°F (180°C).
In a food processor, whirl until just combined
 ¾ cup room-temperature unsalted butter
 1½ cups grated old cheddar
 1 tsp Dijon
Add
 1¼ cups all-purpose flour
 1 tsp coarsely ground black pepper
 ¼ tsp salt
Whirl just until dough forms. Remove and form
into a ball. Pinch off small pieces and roll into
¾-inch (2-cm) balls. Place on an ungreased
baking sheet and flatten until about 1 inch
(2.5 cm) in diameter. Bake in centre of preheated oven until a light golden brown, from
10 to 12 minutes. Cool on a rack.
Makes: 36 small crisps

PREPARATION: 15 MINUTES
BAKING: 12 MINUTES

MAKE AHEAD: Using long sheets of
waxed paper to help with shaping,
form dough into two rolls about
8 inches (20 cm) long and 1 inch
(2.5 cm) in diameter. Roll up and twist paper
ends. Refrigerate for up to a week or over wrap
with foil and freeze for up to a month. Slice
cold rolls about ⅛ inch (0.25 cm) thick and
place on ungreased sheets. Bake as above.

STILTON SHORTBREAD

*This nibbler is adapted from a recipe
by Colleen Walker.*

Preheat oven to 350°F (180°C). Lightly grease
 baking sheets. In a large mixing bowl, using a
 fork, work together until only slightly lumpy
 ¾ cup room-temperature unsalted butter
 1 cup crumbled Stilton cheese
 ¼ tsp salt
Stir in until absorbed
 1¾ cups all-purpose flour
Press into a ball. Pinch off pieces and roll into
 ¾-inch (2-cm) balls. Place on greased baking
 sheets and flatten each until about 1 inch
 (2.5 cm) across. Lightly beat
 1 egg
Brush over tops. Press into tops
 ½ cup coarsely chopped walnuts or pecan
 pieces (optional)
Bake until pale golden, from 10 to 12 minutes.
 Cool on a rack. Store at room temperature
 for up to 3 days or freeze.
Makes: 72 shortbreads

PREPARATION: 15 MINUTES
BAKING: 12 MINUTES

MAKE AHEAD: Using pieces of waxed
paper, form dough into two rolls
about 8 inches (20 cm) long and 1 inch
(2.5 cm) in diameter. Roll up and twist
ends shut. Refrigerate for up to a week or over
wrap with foil and freeze. Slice cold rolls about
⅛ inch (0.25 cm) thick and place on ungreased
baking sheets. Top with a whole nut or chopped
nut pieces. Bake as above.

WONTON NIBBLES

Inexpensive wonton wrappers can be shaped into stylish dippers with just a brief baking. Packages contain two separately wrapped stacks of wrappers so you can conveniently use half a package at a time.

Preheat oven to 375°F (190°C). Open
   I-lb (454-g) pkg wonton wrappers
Brush each wrapper on one side with
   melted butter or olive oil, about ¼ cup total
Stack wrappers after each one is brushed.
Diagonally slice into triangles or long
   continuously cut strips, see diagram (below).
   Place a bit apart on a baking sheet lined with
   slightly crumbled foil.

Bake in centre of preheated oven until bubbled
   and brown spots appear, from 6 to 8 minutes.
   Repeat until all are baked.
Makes: dozens of dippers

> *PREPARATION: 25 MINUTES*
> *BAKING: 8 MINUTES*

VARIATION: FLAVORED NIBBLES
Before baking, sprinkle strips with pinches
of ground cumin, and/or cayenne and dried
parsley. Or brush with dark sesame oil instead
of butter and sprinkle with sesame seeds.

How to make strips

1. Cut wonton in this easy pattern.

2. Lift upper-left corner, then continue
   lifting and let the wonton unravel
   into a long irregular stick.

3. Place on crumbled foil on baking
   sheet and bake according to
   the recipe.

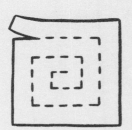
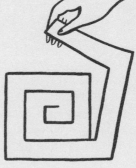

NIBBLES

NIPPY CHEDDAR "GRAPES"

Form these pecan-crusted cheese balls into a cluster of grapes in the centre of a cheese or fruit tray.

In a food processor, whirl until blended
  8-oz (250-g) pkg cream cheese, cut into cubes
  1 lb (500 g) grated sharp cheddar cheese
  1 small minced garlic clove
  2 tbsp sherry
Refrigerate until fairly firm, about 20 minutes. Form rounded teaspoonfuls of cheese into balls. Roll until coated in
  4 cups toasted ground almonds or pecans
Place on a waxed paper-lined tray. Cover with waxed paper and refrigerate for up to a day.
  Makes: 64 "grapes"

PREPARATION: 10 MINUTES
REFRIGERATION: 20 MINUTES

MAKE AHEAD: Layer "grapes" between sheets of waxed paper in a sealed container and refrigerate for up to a week.

SPICY FRUIT 'N' NUTS

Warm spiced nuts couldn't be easier than this baked number.

Preheat oven to 350°F (180°C). Toss together
  2 cups unblanched almonds or pecans
  1 tbsp olive oil
Spread on a baking sheet. Toast in preheated oven for 5 minutes. Sprinkle with
  ½ tsp cumin
  ½ tsp cinnamon
  ¼ tsp chili powder
  ¼ tsp cayenne
Toss, then toast for 5 more minutes. Stir in
  ½ cup raisins
  Makes: 2½ cups

PREPARATION: 5 MINUTES
BAKING: 10 MINUTES

Nippy Cheddar "Grapes"

HOT TUNA MUSHROOMS

Jalapeños give unexpected heat to these easy-to-make nibblers.

Preheat oven to 375°F (190°C).
Stir together
  6.5-oz (184-g) can drained flaked tuna
  ½ cup room-temperature cream cheese
  2 tbsp finely chopped jalapeños
  pinch of pepper
Fill about
  36 large mushroom caps
Bake on a cookie sheet until hot, about 5 minutes.
  Makes: 36 mushroom caps

> *PREPARATION: 10 MINUTES*
> *BAKING: 5 MINUTES*

MAKE AHEAD: Stuffed unbaked mushrooms will keep well for 3 to 4 hours in the refrigerator.

SPICY OLIVES

This pretty and fiery mélange of olives is perfect for nibbling with a glass of robust red wine.

Stir together
  3 cups, about 1 lb (500 g), drained mixed green
    and black olives, such as cracked green,
    Kalamata and wine-cured black olives
  finely grated peel of 1 lemon
  1 tbsp lemon juice
  1 tbsp olive oil
  ½ to 1 tsp Harissa or chili-garlic sauce
    or other hot pepper sauce
Cover and marinate 1 hour at room temperature
  or refrigerate overnight. Then drain olives
  and stir in
  ¼ cup chopped fresh parsley or coriander
  Makes: 3 cups

> *PREPARATION: 10 MINUTES*
> *MARINATING: 1 HOUR*

MARINATED MUSHROOMS

Let these irresistible nibblers star in an antipasto buffet or team with grilled steak.

In a large bowl, whisk together
  1 cup olive oil
  ⅓ cup balsamic vinegar
  ½ tsp dry mustard
  2 minced garlic cloves
  3 thinly sliced green onions
  2 tbsp finely chopped fresh tarragon
    or 1 tsp dried tarragon
Stir in
  1 lb (500 g) very small mushrooms,
    or large ones cut in half
  1 chopped red pepper
  2 thinly sliced green onions
  ¼ cup chopped fresh parsley
Leave at room temperature for 30 minutes,
  stirring frequently, before serving.
  Makes: 8 servings

> *PREPARATION: 15 MINUTES*
> *STANDING: 30 MINUTES*

MAKE AHEAD: Prepare and refrigerate for up to a day.

CARAMEL CORN

Microwave your favorite popcorn, then "caramelize" it with this toss and bake.

Preheat oven to 350°F (180°C). Stir together
  3 tbsp melted butter
  ¼ cup brown sugar
  ½ tsp cinnamon
  ½ tsp allspice
Toss with
  8 cups popcorn
Spread on a baking sheet. Bake in preheated
  oven, stirring occasionally, 5 minutes.
  Makes: 8 cups

> *PREPARATION: 5 MINUTES*

RISOTTOS

Golden squash with harvest seasonings gives a rich body to this creamy EARLY AUTUMN RISOTTO (see recipe page 90) – perfect for starting a Thanksgiving dinner.

EARLY AUTUMN RISOTTO

A creamy squash risotto makes an elegant beginning for a harvest dinner.
For a perfect vegetarian dinner, use vegetable broth.

Pierce
    I small acorn squash or butternut squash

Place in the microwave. Cook, on high, until
    soft enough to cut, about 4 minutes for
    acorn, 6 minutes for butternut. Remove
    from microwave. Slice in half. Discard seeds
    and peel. Slice into ½-inch (1-cm) cubes.

In a wide saucepan over medium heat, melt
    I tbsp butter

Add squash cubes and
    I minced garlic clove
    ¼ tsp cayenne pepper

Stir-fry for 5 minutes. Then remove to a bowl.
    Add to saucepan and stir-fry for 3 minutes
    I chopped seeded large sweet pepper

Remove to another bowl. Don't add to squash.
    Add to pan another
    I tbsp butter

When hot, add
    I finely chopped onion
    2 minced garlic cloves

Sauté, stirring often, until onion has softened,
    about 5 minutes. Then add another
    I tbsp butter

When melted, add
    I cup short-grain rice, preferably Arborio

Stir until rice is slightly translucent, about
    2 minutes. While constantly stirring, add
    ½ cup dry white wine
    2 tsp cumin
    ½ tsp mace
    ¼ tsp salt

Stir gently until rice has absorbed wine. Then
    add another
    ½ cup dry white wine

Stir until absorbed. Gradually stir in ¼ cup
    at a time
    2 (10-oz/284-mL) cans undiluted
      chicken broth
    ½ cup water

Stir frequently after each addition of liquid
    and wait until almost all liquid is absorbed
    before adding next amount. This process is
    necessary to achieve creaminess. Continue
    additions until all liquid has been added.
    Add squash. Then add ¼ cup at a time
    2 cups water

Stir frequently until most of water is absorbed
    before adding more.

When rice is just tender to the bite, stir
    in peppers and
    I sliced small zucchini
    ½ to I cup Parmesan
    ½ cup coarsely chopped fresh coriander
      or parsley

Serve right away.
    Makes: 6 appetizer servings

PREPARATION: 20 MINUTES
COOKING: 45 MINUTES

SPRING RISOTTO WITH CHÈVRE

Distinctive chèvre gives richness and zing to this creamy risotto – a perfect light spring starter.

In a wide saucepan over medium heat, melt
   1 tbsp butter
When bubbly, add
   2 minced garlic cloves
Stir often until fragrant, about 1 minute.
   Then stir in until coated
   1 cup short-grain rice, preferably Arborio
While constantly stirring, add
   1 cup dry white wine
   ¼ to ½ tsp hot red pepper flakes
Stir gently until rice absorbs wine. Then gradually
   stir in ¼ cup at a time
   10-oz (284-mL) can undiluted chicken broth
   1½ cups water
Stir frequently after each addition of liquid
   and wait until almost all liquid is absorbed

before adding next amount. Continue ¼ cup additions until all liquid has been added. The cooking-and-stirring process takes at least 25 minutes. With last addition of liquid, add
   1 to 2 bunches asparagus, sliced into
   ½-inch (1-cm) pieces
Continue stirring often, until asparagus is cooked. Mixture should be soupy. Then stir in
   4.5-oz (140-g) pkg creamy goat cheese,
   about ½ cup
   3 to 4 thinly sliced green onions
Makes: 6 appetizer servings

PREPARATION: 15 MINUTES
COOKING: 35 MINUTES

SPRING RISOTTO WITH CHÈVRE

RISOTTOS

NO-WATCH THANKSGIVING RISOTTO

*While canned pumpkin pie filling makes a nice pie,
look for "pure pumpkin" for this recipe.*

In a 12-cup bowl or dish, place
  1 tbsp butter
Microwave on high until melted, about
  30 seconds. Stir in until coated
  1 cup short-grain rice, preferably Arborio
Microwave, covered, for 2 minutes. Add
  1 cup canned pure pumpkin
  10-oz (284-mL) can undiluted
    chicken broth
  2 soup cans water
  ½ tsp each salt, nutmeg and dry leaf thyme
Mix well. Cover tightly and microwave on high
  for 20 minutes. Stir and microwave on high
  for 5 minutes. Stir again. Then microwave on
  high for 5 minutes longer or until rice is
  tender. Stir in
  ¼ cup dry white wine
  ½ cup freshly grated Parmesan
  2 thinly sliced green onions
Then for a truly creamy risotto, stir in
  ¼ cup homogenized milk or table cream
    (optional)
Serve right away.
  Makes: 6 appetizer servings

  PREPARATION: 15 MINUTES
  COOKING: 32 MINUTES

BROCCOLI RISOTTO

*There's textural interplay between slightly crunchy
broccolini and creamy rice in this flavorful risotto.*

In a large wide saucepan over medium, melt
  1 tbsp butter
When bubbly, add
  2 minced garlic cloves
Sauté, stirring often until fragrant, about
  1 minute. Then add
  1 cup short-grain rice, preferably Arborio
Stir until rice is slightly translucent, about
  2 minutes. While constantly stirring, add
  1 cup dry white wine
  ¼ to ½ tsp hot red pepper flakes
Stir gently until rice has absorbed wine.
Gradually stir in ¼ cup at a time
  10-oz (284-mL) can undiluted chicken broth
  1½ to 1¾ cups water
Stir frequently after each addition of liquid
  and wait until almost all liquid is absorbed
  before adding next amount. This process
  is necessary to achieve creaminess. After
  10 minutes of cooking, stir in
  2 cups chopped broccoli
    or 1 coarsely chopped bunch broccolini
Continue liquid additions until a total of
  1½ cups water have been added, from
  15 to 20 more minutes. Stir in
  10 finely chopped large fresh basil leaves
  ½ cup freshly grated Parmesan
  2 chopped seeded large ripe plum tomatoes
  3 to 4 thinly sliced green onions
Stir in another ¼ cup water if needed. Serve
  right away.
  Makes: 6 appetizer servings

  PREPARATION: 15 MINUTES
  COOKING: 30 MINUTES

SEAFOOD RISOTTO WITH PEAS

*With its scallops and shrimp, this creamy risotto is truly an impressive
way to begin a dinner party.*

Rinse with cold water and pat dry
   ¼ lb (125 g) each small bay scallops and
      peeled fresh or frozen shrimp
In a large wide saucepan over medium, heat
   1 tbsp butter
Add
   1 finely chopped small onion
   3 minced large garlic cloves
Sauté, stirring often, until onion has softened,
   about 5 minutes. Add another
   1 tbsp butter
   1 cup short-grain rice, preferably Arborio
Stir until rice is slightly translucent, about
   2 minutes. While constantly stirring, add
   ½ cup dry white wine
   ½ tsp salt
   ¼ tsp cayenne (optional)
Stir gently until rice has absorbed wine. Then
   add another
   ½ cup dry white wine
Stir until absorbed. Gradually stir in ¼ cup
   at a time
   10-oz (284-mL) can undiluted chicken broth
   3½ to 4 cups water

Stir frequently after each addition of liquid and
   wait until almost all liquid is absorbed before
   adding next amount. This process achieves
   creaminess. Continue ¼ cup additions until
   all liquid has been added. The cooking-and-
   stirring process takes at least 35 minutes.
   When rice is almost tender to the bite, very
   creamy and still a little soupy, stir in shrimp,
   scallops and
   1 cup fresh or frozen peas
Continue stirring often until shrimp are bright
   pink and peas are hot, about 5 minutes.
   Then stir in
   ½ cup freshly grated Parmesan
   ½ cup coarsely chopped fresh parsley
      or coriander
Serve with lemon wedges if you wish. Risotto is
   best served right away.
   Makes: 6 appetizer servings

   PREPARATION: 20 MINUTES
   COOKING: 40 MINUTES

TIPS

The Rice Stuff

Look for short, fat and starchy rice to make
a creamy risotto. During a risotto's long
simmering and constant stirring, the starch
helps to form a sauce so creamy that it is hard
to believe no whipping cream has been added.
Arborio, named for a village in the Piedmont
region of Italy, is the most widely available short-
grain rice. The best quality is labeled superfino,
followed by fino and then semifino. Less widely
available, though often preferred over Arborio,
are carnaroli and vialone nano. Store rice in a
cool dry spot.

SALADS

Serve this CURRY-SPINACH SALAD (see recipe page 96) with hot bread sticks or focaccia.

SALADS

CURRY-SPINACH SALAD

Indian spices punch up the flavor in this interesting twist on a popular salad from artist Leisa Temple.

Whisk together
   3 tbsp vegetable oil
   2 tbsp freshly squeezed lemon juice
   ½ tsp granulated sugar
   ¼ tsp each curry powder and salt
Measure out
   2 tbsp mango chutney
Finely chop any large chunks in chutney.
   Stir into dressing. In a large salad bowl,
   toss together
   2 bunches fresh spinach or 10-oz (284-g) bag
     spinach, torn into bite-size pieces
   1 cored sliced apple
Toss with dressing and scatter with
   ⅓ thinly sliced red onion
   ¼ cup toasted sunflower seeds or slivered
     almonds (optional)
   Makes: 4 to 6 servings

PREPARATION: 15 MINUTES

MAKE AHEAD: Up to half a day ahead, wash, dry, cover and refrigerate spinach. Make dressing and leave at room temperature. When ready to serve, toss with cored sliced apple, red onion and seeds.

COUNTRY SPINACH SALAD

This is a great starter salad when steak and baked potato are on the menu.

Whisk together
   ¼ cup olive or vegetable oil
   2 tbsp balsamic vinegar
   1 tbsp liquid honey
   ¼ tsp dried leaf tarragon
   pinches of salt and black pepper
In a large salad bowl, toss together
   2 bunches fresh spinach or 10-oz (284-g) bag
     spinach, torn into bite-size pieces
   ¼ lb (125 g) sliced mushrooms
   ¼ lb (125 g) grated Asiago or Fontina cheese
Toss with dressing and scatter over top
   ½ thinly sliced small red onion
   Makes: 6 servings

PREPARATION: 15 MINUTES

MAKE AHEAD: Dressing can be covered and refrigerated for up to 1 week.

MARINATED MUSHROOM SALAD

Consider this salad with tasty mushrooms to begin a family barbecue.

Toss together
   2 cups sliced mushrooms
   2 to 3 tbsp vinaigrette or Italian dressing
   2 tbsp chopped fresh basil
     or ½ tsp dried basil
Taste and add
   pinches of salt and ground black pepper
Serve on
   bed of lettuce
Scatter with
   chopped tomato or red pepper
   Makes: 4 to 5 appetizer salads

PREPARATION: 5 MINUTES

TOMATO SALAD WITH ARTICHOKE DRESSING

Fragrant fresh basil and succulent vine-ripened tomatoes need little adornment in this simple salad.

In a food processor, whirl
  ½ cup lightly packed fresh basil leaves
  14-oz (398-mL) can drained artichoke hearts
  1 minced garlic clove
  1 tbsp each lemon juice and olive oil
With processor running, slowly add
  ½ to ¾ cup buttermilk
Tear into bite-size pieces
  1 head romaine or leaf lettuce or 8 cups
    mixed greens

Arrange equally on individual salad plates. Slice
  4 large beefsteak tomatoes
  4 hard-boiled eggs
Arrange tomatoes over greens. Place eggs
  decoratively on top of tomatoes.
Drizzle with dressing.
Serve with focaccia or corn bread.
  Makes: 4 servings

PREPARATION: 10 MINUTES

TOMATO SALAD WITH ARTICHOKE DRESSING

FRESH BEET, SPINACH & ORANGE SALAD

This very colorful salad is a perfect starter for a fall dinner. And the beets, orange and spinach are beautiful together.

Place in a saucepan filled with water
> 3 unpeeled medium-size beets with stems trimmed

Cover and bring to a boil. Then reduce heat and boil gently for 25 to 30 minutes, until beets are tender but still firm.

Meanwhile, in a small bowl, whisk together
> ¼ cup olive oil
> 1 tbsp cider vinegar
> 1 tsp Dijon
> finely grated peel of 1 orange
> ¼ tsp each salt and freshly ground black pepper

Stir in
> 2 tbsp chopped fresh dill or ½ tsp dried dillweed

In a large bowl, place
> 1 bunch fresh spinach, torn into bite-size pieces
> 1 peeled orange, sliced and quartered

Drain beets and rinse under cold water. Slip off skins. Trim off any remaining stem, then thinly slice beets. Toss spinach and orange segments with half the dressing. Place on salad plates. Scatter beets over salad. Drizzle with a little more dressing. Sprinkle with
> 2 tbsp toasted pine nuts

Makes: 4 to 6 servings

PREPARATION: 20 MINUTES
COOKING: 30 MINUTES

Fresh Beet, Spinach & Orange Salad

WARM SPINACH & CHÈVRE SALAD

*This is the perfect beginner or companion dish
for your next special dinner for two.*

On a microwave-safe plate, place
   2 slices bacon, cut into ½-inch (1-cm) pieces
Microwave on high, uncovered and stirring
   once, until crisp, 2 minutes.
In a small bowl, pour
   1 tsp bacon fat
Whisk in
   2 tsp olive oil
   1 tsp balsamic or red wine vinegar
   pinches of salt and black pepper
Warm in microwave, uncovered, on high,
   30 seconds. Pour over
   3 cups spinach, torn into bite-size pieces
Toss until coated, then sprinkle with bacon and
   ¼ cup crumbled creamy goat cheese
Makes: 2 first-course servings

   PREPARATION: 10 MINUTES
   MICROWAVING: 2½ MINUTES

MAKE AHEAD: Prepare dressing to the
point of warming and leave at room
temperature for up to a day. Prepare
greens and refrigerate for up to a day.

RADICCHIO & SPINACH SALAD

*Warm toasted pecans tossed into a simple
vinaigrette create an extremely sophisticated salad.*

In a small dry frying pan over medium-low, heat
   ½ cup pecan halves
Heat until fragrant and toasted, about
   5 minutes. Meanwhile, in a small bowl,
   whisk together
   3 tbsp olive oil
   1 tbsp red wine vinegar
   1 tsp brown sugar
   1 tsp maple syrup
   ¼ tsp salt
When nuts are toasted, set aside half to use as
   garnish. Coarsely chop remaining and stir
   into vinaigrette. In a small salad bowl,
   combine
   1 small head radicchio, torn into small
     bite-size pieces
   10-oz (284-g) bag baby spinach,
     about 7 cups when loosened
Spoon warm dressing over top and toss
   until leaves glisten. Serve right away in
   individual salad bowls or plates sprinkled
   with remaining pecan halves.
Makes: 6 servings

   PREPARATION: 10 MINUTES
   COOKING: 5 MINUTES

SALADS

WARM MUSHROOM SALAD

Mix and match whatever mushrooms you like for this salad. Portobello is good for a meaty richness.

In a large frying pan over medium-high, heat
    2 tbsp olive oil
Add
    4 cups sliced mushrooms
Sauté until lightly browned, about 10 minutes.
Then stir together
    1 tbsp white wine vinegar
    ½ tsp Dijon
    pinches of salt and black pepper
Stir into browned mushrooms. Remove from
    heat. Immediately toss with
    4 cups mixed greens
Serve sprinkled with
    ¼ cup crumbled Stilton or feta cheese
    Makes: 4 small salads

PREPARATION: 10 MINUTES

PEACHES & FRESH MINT SALAD

Peaches are a passion food. Combined here with mint, they make a refreshing starter.

In a large bowl, stir together
    ½ cup light mayonnaise
    ¼ cup orange juice
    2 tbsp chopped fresh mint or ½ tsp dried mint
Stir in
    4 sliced peaches
Tear into bite-size pieces
    1 head Boston lettuce
Arrange equally on individual salad plates.
    Spoon dressing and peaches over top.
    Makes: 4 to 6 servings

PREPARATION: 5 MINUTES

RED PEPPER & PINE NUT SALAD

Roasted sweet red peppers and pine nuts give delicious character to this distinctive salad.

Preheat broiler. Place a piece of foil on a baking
    sheet. Lightly oil
    2 large red peppers
Place on foil and broil, turning as skin blackens,
    about 15 minutes. Seal in foil and let sit for
    5 minutes. Then peel off blackened skin
    and seed peppers. Slice into strips. In a small
    bowl, whisk together
    ⅓ cup olive oil
    3 tbsp freshly squeezed lemon juice
    1 tsp Dijon
    ¼ tsp each salt, freshly ground black pepper
    and dried basil
In a large salad bowl, toss pepper strips and
    dressing with
    1 head romaine lettuce, torn into
    bite-size pieces
    ½ cup toasted pine nuts
Sprinkle with
    curls of Parmesan
Serve right away.
    Makes: 8 servings

PREPARATION: 10 MINUTES
BROILING: 15 MINUTES

MAKE AHEAD: Prepare peppers and dressing up to a day ahead and leave at room temperature. Combine lettuce and pine nuts and refrigerate.

Celeriac Salad

*Crunch and a refreshing celery taste give a unique no-wilt quality to this upscale salad.
It's an ideal one to make ahead for a posh party.*

As soon as it is cut, blanch in a pot of boiling
water for just 1 minute
  1 celeriac, peeled and julienned
Drain and rinse under cold running water until
cold. Drain well and place in a large bowl. In
another bowl, whisk together
  3 tbsp olive oil
  1 tbsp freshly squeezed lemon juice
  ½ tsp dried basil
  ¼ tsp dried leaf oregano
  ⅛ tsp salt
  pinch of freshly ground black pepper

Toss with celeriac. Add
  2 chopped seeded tomatoes
Serve on mixed greens.
  Makes: 6 servings

PREPARATION: 20 MINUTES
COOKING: 1 MINUTE

MAKE AHEAD: Toss dressing with
celeriac and refrigerate for up to a day.
Add tomatoes just before serving.

CELERIAC SALAD

SALADS

CREOLE SALAD

There's lots of bold southern flavors in this green pepper salad. Perfect with grilled fish.

Whisk together
   ¼ cup vegetable oil
   2 tbsp white vinegar
   2 tbsp chopped fresh basil or 1 tsp dried basil
   ⅛ tsp each garlic powder, onion powder,
      dried leaf thyme, cayenne, salt and
      black pepper
In a large bowl, toss together
   3 seeded green peppers, cut into 1-inch
      (2.5-cm) pieces
   1 thinly sliced onion
   3 sliced celery stalks
   2 tomatoes, cut into wedges
   ¼ cup each sliced black olives
      and pimento-stuffed green olives
Toss with dressing.
   Makes: 6 servings

PREPARATION: 20 MINUTES

MAKE AHEAD: Covered and refrigerated, salad will keep well for 2 days.

CHILI JICAMA SALAD

Jicama is a popular Tex-Mex vegetable that is crunchy and mildy sweet like a water chestnut.

Peel and thinly slice into matchstick-size pieces
   1 small jicama or bunch of celery
Cut off peel and white membrane from
   4 oranges
Slice about ½ inch (1 cm) thick and cut
   into quarters.
Combine with jicama or celery in a large bowl.
   Add
   4 thinly sliced green onions
   ¼ to ½ thinly sliced red or Vidalia onion

In a small bowl, whisk together
   juice of 1 lime
   2 tbsp vegetable oil
   1 tsp Dijon
   2 tsp liquid honey or granulated sugar
   ½ tsp salt
   1 finely chopped seeded jalapeño
      or ¼ to ½ tsp hot red pepper flakes
When well blended, pour over jicama mixture.
   Stir until coated. Serve right away for best
   flavor on
   a bed of sliced lettuce or mixed salad greens
   Makes: 5 to 6 servings

PREPARATION: 15 MINUTES

MANDARIN HONEY SALAD

This is a perfect starter salad to accompany roasted Cornish hens or barbecued chicken.

Whisk together
   ¼ cup vegetable oil
   2 tbsp rice wine vinegar
   finely grated peel of 1 small orange
   2 tbsp freshly squeezed orange juice
   1 tbsp liquid honey
   1½ tsp Dijon
In a large salad bowl, combine
   1 large head butter or Boston lettuce,
      torn into bite-size pieces
   ½ thinly sliced small red onion
   ½ cup well-drained mandarin orange slices
   1 to 2 tbsp drained capers
Toss with dressing.
Sprinkle with
   2 tbsp coarsely chopped walnuts
      or hazelnuts (optional)
   Makes: 4 servings

PREPARATION: 10 MINUTES

Strawberry Spinach Salad

Here's an "I don't feel like cooking" summer salad from Samantha Thiessen, packed with calcium and vitamin C.

In a small bowl, whisk together
- 2 tbsp each low-fat mayonnaise and low-fat plain yogurt or light sour cream
- ¼ cup orange juice
- ½ tsp sugar

In a small salad bowl, combine
- 1 to 2 bunches fresh spinach or 10-oz (284-g) bag baby spinach, torn into bite-size pieces, about 7 cups when loosened
- 2 cups sliced fresh strawberries

Toss with dressing. For extra crunch, lightly sprinkle with
- poppy seeds or toasted sliced almonds (optional)

Makes: 6 to 8 servings

PREPARATION: 15 MINUTES

MAKE AHEAD: Prepare spinach and dressing. Cover separately and refrigerate for up to a day. When ready to serve, slice strawberries and add to spinach. Whisk dressing well before tossing with salad. Sprinkle with poppy seeds or almonds.

STRAWBERRY SPINACH SALAD

SALADS

CELERIAC WITH BEETS & APPLE

Mild celery-flavored celeriac joins earthy beets and sweet apples in this intriguing salad.

Bring a large pot of water to a boil.
In a large bowl, whisk together
   3 tbsp vegetable or olive oil
   2 tbsp freshly squeezed lemon juice
   1 tsp Dijon
   1 tsp liquid honey or sugar
   ¼ cup chopped fresh dill
     or ¼ to ½ tsp dried dillweed
   ¼ tsp each salt and pepper
Using a peeler or sharp chef's knife, peel
   1 celeriac
Cut into quarters, then very thinly slice in a food processor. Add to boiling water. Once water returns to boil, drain immediately and refresh under cold running water. Toss with dressing until evenly coated. Rub skins off
   4 cooked medium beets
     or 14-oz (398-mL) can baby beets
Add to celeriac with
   1 peeled quartered green apple
Toss until evenly coated.
Makes: 4 to 6 servings

PREPARATION: 20 MINUTES

MAKE AHEAD: Covered and refrigerated, salad will keep well for up to a day.

PEACH & TARRAGON SALAD

For this elegant salad from food stylist Ettie Shuken, assemble the components and serve when needed.

Preheat oven to 400°C (200°C). On a flat baking sheet, place
   ½ cup sliced almonds or nuts, such as pecans, hazelnuts or macadamia
Toast from 4 to 5 minutes, stirring twice until fragrant and a pale tan color. Cool.
Divide into six portions
   4.5-oz (140-g) pkg creamy goat cheese, about ½ cup
Flatten into ½-inch (1-cm) thick disks. Dip each round into almonds and gently pat nuts into surface. All the almonds may not be used.
In a small bowl, whisk together
   4 tbsp vegetable or olive oil
   2 tbsp cider vinegar
   1 tsp Dijon
   2 tsp liquid honey
   ¼ tsp salt
   1½ tsp dried tarragon
Divide equally onto six serving plates
   9 cups mesclun or other salad greens (see New Salad Days, page 113)
Slice
   3 peaches, nectarines or pears or 6 plums
Divide fruit equally among plates. Place nut-covered chèvre rounds in the centre. Drizzle with dressing and serve right away.
Makes: 6 servings

PREPARATION: 15 MINUTES

MAKE AHEAD: Up to half a day ahead, prepare nut-covered chèvre rounds. Cover and refrigerate. Prepare dressing and leave at room temperature. Wash greens, spin dry. Cover with a damp paper towel and refrigerate. Bring cheese rounds to room temperature about an hour before serving. Slice peaches just before assembling salad.

SOUTHERN HONEY-LIME FRUIT SALAD

A touch of dry mustard intensifies tequila's wallop of flavor. The marinade is so good, you could use it poured over crushed ice for sipping.

In a small bowl, whisk together
- ¼ cup freshly squeezed lime juice
- ¼ cup liquid honey
- ¼ cup tequila, rum or bourbon
- ½ tsp dry mustard
- ¼ tsp salt

In a large bowl, place
- 4 cups fresh fruit chunks, such as melon, pineapple, mango or strawberries

Pour in dressing and stir until coated. Let sit at room temperature, stirring occasionally, to develop flavors at least 1 hour or up to 3 hours.

Makes: 4 cups

PREPARATION: 20 MINUTES
MARINATING: 1 HOUR

MAKE AHEAD: Covered and refrigerated, salad keeps well for up to half a day.

FRUIT TIP:
Sturdy fruit like pineapple chunks, mango slices or firm strawberries hold very well for hours and are a good choice for the base of this salad. If using soft fruits like melons, peaches, raspberries, blueberries or bananas, add about an hour before serving.

SALADS

SOUTHERN HONEY-LIME FRUIT SALAD

SALADS

Bacon & Spinach Salad

*This combo, along with mushrooms, is becoming
a classic. This version is one of the best.*

In a large heat-proof bowl, place
  2 bunches fresh spinach or 10-oz (284-g) bag
    spinach, torn into bite-size pieces
In a frying pan, over medium heat, cook until
  crisp, about 5 minutes
  ¼ lb (125 g) diced bacon
Drain bacon bits, but leave fat in pan. Add
  ½ cup slivered almonds
Stir often until golden, about 5 minutes. Remove
  with a slotted spoon and set aside with bacon.
  To fat in pan, add
  ½ lb (250 g) sliced mushrooms
Sauté for 4 minutes. Push to side of pan. Add
  ¼ cup balsamic vinegar
Reduce by half, about 2 minutes. Whisk in
  2 tbsp Dijon
Remove from heat. Immediately add to spinach
  and toss until coated. Scatter with bacon and
  almonds. Cover salad bowl with hot frying
  pan for 1 minute just until spinach begins to
  wilt. Sprinkle with
  ½ cup grated Parmesan
  pinches of salt and black pepper
Serve right away.
  Makes: 8 first-course servings

  PREPARATION: 10 MINUTES
  COOKING: 15 MINUTES

Sensational Shrimp Starter Salad

*Make this intriguing salad with cooked salad
shrimp from the deli section of your supermarket.*

Whisk together
  ¼ cup freshly squeezed lemon juice
  2 tbsp red wine vinegar
  1 minced garlic clove
  1 tsp dried leaf oregano
  ½ tsp granulated sugar
  ¼ tsp each freshly ground black pepper,
    salt and Worcestershire
Slowly whisk in
  ½ cup olive oil
In a large salad bowl, toss together
  2 heads Bibb lettuce, torn into
    bite-size pieces
  2 tomatoes, cut into wedges
  8 sliced mushrooms
  12 oz (375 g) small cooked salad shrimp
    or frozen salad shrimp, rinsed and drained
Drizzle with about half the dressing and toss.
  Taste and add more dressing if needed.
Sprinkle with
  1 grated hard-boiled egg
Serve immediately.
  Makes: 4 to 6 first-course servings

  PREPARATION: 20 MINUTES

MAKE AHEAD: Dressing can be covered
and refrigerated for up to a week.

New Shrimp Cocktail Salad

Shallots, tangy salsa and fresh dill give a trendy touch to this interesting starter salad.
Serve it in large martini glasses for a chic touch.

Whisk together
- 1/3 cup olive oil
- 2 tbsp freshly squeezed lemon juice
- 1 tsp Dijon
- 1 1/2 tbsp finely chopped shallots
- 1/4 tsp each salt, sugar and freshly ground black pepper

In a small bowl, stir 2 tbsp of dressing with
- 2 tbsp salsa

Then stir in
- 1 lb (500 g) cold cooked medium or large shrimp

In a large salad bowl, toss together
- 1 large head Bibb lettuce, torn into bite-size pieces
- 1/2 English cucumber, finely chopped
- 2 thinly sliced green onions
- 1/4 cup coarsely chopped fresh dill

Toss with remaining dressing until evenly coated. Divide among serving plates, top with shrimp and scatter with
- 2 tbsp coarsely chopped fresh dill

Makes: 8 appetizer servings

PREPARATION: 20 MINUTES

MAKE AHEAD: Dressing can be covered and refrigerated for several days and lettuce and shrimp mixture for half a day.

New Shrimp Cocktail Salad

SALADS

FRENCH MUSSEL SALAD

*Mussels are inexpensive as seafood goes.
Here they become an elegant salad.*

In a large wide saucepan, bring to a boil over
medium-high heat
½ cup white wine
¼ tsp dried leaf thyme

Scrub under cold water and remove any
beards from
3 lbs (1.5 kg) mussels

Discard any mussels that are open and will not
close when gently tapped. Then add mussels
to boiling white wine mixture.

Cover and cook until mussels are open, from
5 to 8 minutes. Discard any that aren't
open. Remove from heat and refrigerate
mussels to cool quickly. Place 1 tbsp wine-
cooking liquid in a small bowl, then stir in
3 tbsp sour cream
3 tbsp mayonnaise
1 tsp Dijon
2 tbsp chopped fresh chives
pinches of salt and black pepper

Remove mussels from shells, discarding
liquid, and toss with dressing. Refrigerate
until chilled.

Serve on lettuce as a first course or with
toothpicks as an appetizer.

Makes: 4 first-course servings

> *PREPARATION: 20 MINUTES*
> *COOKING: 8 MINUTES*

MAKE AHEAD: Salad can be covered
and refrigerated for up to half a day.

ELEGANT SEAFOOD SALAD

*Saffron, white wine and shallots elevate this salad
to haute cuisine – sure to impress.*

In a large saucepan, bring to a boil
juice of 1 orange
2 tbsp finely chopped shallots
¾ cup dry white wine
grinding of white pepper

Add
1 lb (500 g) fresh or frozen uncooked peeled
medium-sized shrimp

Cover and simmer until shrimp turn pink, about
2 to 4 minutes. Remove shrimp and add
½ lb (250 g) scallops, preferably smaller
bay scallops

Cover and simmer until opaque, about
3 minutes. Remove scallops. Refrigerate
seafood, uncovered, on paper towels. Then
add to cooking liquid
grated peel of 1 orange
1 tsp saffron threads

Boil over medium-high heat until reduced to
about ⅓ cup, about 10 minutes. Strain,
discarding solids. Place liquid in freezer to
chill. When cold, whisk together with
½ cup mayonnaise
2 thinly sliced green onions
1 tbsp chopped pimento
pinch of cayenne

Stir in chilled seafood. Serve right away or cover
and refrigerate for up to half a day.

Serve on a bed of soft-leaf lettuce. Looks great
in martini glasses.

Makes: 8 appetizer servings

> *PREPARATION: 20 MINUTES*
> *COOKING: 20 MINUTES*

MAKE AHEAD: Salad can be covered
and refrigerated for up to half a day.

CARIBBEAN SHRIMP CAESAR

Stir-fried island-spiced shrimp and juicy mango mingle in a creamy dressing in this great salad.
The shrimp are tossed still hot with the cool greens.

In a large salad bowl, place
    1 head romaine lettuce, torn into
      bite-size pieces
Measure out and have ready
    1 mango, peeled and diced
Rinse with cold water and pat dry
    1 lb (500 g) fresh or frozen peeled shrimp
In a large nonstick frying pan over medium
    heat, melt
    1 tbsp butter
Add shrimp. Sprinkle with
    ¼ tsp each allspice, cinnamon and cayenne

Stir-fry just until shrimp are bright pink and hot,
    from 3 to 5 minutes. Then squeeze over top
    ½ lime
Remove from heat. Immediately toss
    romaine with
    ⅓ to ½ cup creamy Caesar dressing
Add
    ¼ cup freshly grated Parmesan
Then add mango and warm shrimp mixture.
    Toss and serve right away.
    Makes: 4 to 6 first-course servings

        PREPARATION: 20 MINUTES
        COOKING: 5 MINUTES

CARIBBEAN SHRIMP CAESAR

SALADS

Salad Dressings

Here are some jazzy dressings to add to your repertoire.

Lemon Italian Parmesan

In a jar, combine
   1/4 cup freshly grated Parmesan
   1/4 cup olive oil
   1 tbsp freshly squeezed lemon juice
   1 minced garlic clove
   1/2 to 1 tsp dried basil
   1/4 tsp each dried leaf oregano
      and black pepper
Shake until blended.
Toss with sliced zucchini and spinach.
   Makes: 1/2 cup

Sassy Stilton

In a blender, whirl together
   1/2 cup crumbled Stilton or blue cheese
   2 tbsp milk
   1 tbsp freshly squeezed lemon juice
      or white vinegar
   1 sliced green onion
   1/4 tsp black pepper
If necessary, thin with 2 tbsp milk, adding
   1 tbsp at a time. Toss with crisp greens
   or drizzle over sliced pears on lettuce.
   Makes: 1/3 cup

Warm Goat Cheese

In a microwave-safe bowl, place about
   1/4 cup creamy goat cheese
   2 tbsp olive or vegetable oil
   1 tsp white vinegar
   1/4 tsp each black pepper and dried leaf thyme
Microwave, uncovered, on medium for
   30 seconds. Whisk until blended.
   Toss immediately with greens.
   Makes: 1/3 cup

Light Mediterranean

In a blender, whirl
   1/2 cup feta cheese
   2 tbsp milk
   1 tbsp each freshly squeezed lemon juice
      and olive oil
   1/2 tsp each dried leaf oregano and dried basil
Thin, if necessary, with milk, about 1 tbsp
   at a time. Toss with tomatoes, black olives
   and lettuce.
   Makes: 1/2 cup

Sesame Ginger

Whisk
   1/4 cup vegetable oil
   1 tbsp sesame oil
   1 tbsp freshly squeezed lime juice
   1 tbsp soy sauce
   2 minced garlic cloves
   1/4 tsp each sugar and grated fresh ginger
   a pinch of cayenne
Toss with cold Oriental noodles and sliced
   vegetables or spinach and artichokes.
   Makes: 1/2 cup

TIPS

New Salad Days

There was a time when salad was simply iceberg lettuce, grated carrot, tomato wedges and bottled Thousand Island dressing. Today, there are a wide variety of greens available.

Experiment with different combinations of greens. Soft buttery Bibb or Boston lettuce is complemented by sharp endive or peppery watercress. Delicate loose leaf lettuce looks and tastes great with crunchy radicchio. Here are some greens to try:

- Arugula is related to the mustard family. It can be very peppery. It's usually sold in bunches with the roots attached. Look for small bright-green leaves that resemble radish leaves and long thin stalks.

- Chard is derived from the beet family. Look for crinkly green leaves and celery-like stalks. One variety is reddish, and has strong flavor and dark-green leaves. The leaves taste similar to spinach.

- Endive is generally bitter. There are three main varieties: Belgian endive is cream-colored with yellow-green tips, has tightly packed leaves and is cigar-shaped; curly endive has pale stalks with darker green tips, very curly, loose leaves and an almost prickly texture; and escarole is pale to dark green with slightly curvy broad leaves and a mild flavor.

- Mesclun is a mixture of young salad greens such as baby spinach, frisée, arugula, oak leaf and radicchio. Together they deliver a fresh yet bitter and tangy flavor combined with a smooth and frilled texture. The mixture is often labeled as a salad mix or baby greens and is sold loose by the pound (kilogram) in grocery produce sections. For an economical but still interesting approach, mix an equal amount of mesclun greens with torn Boston, leaf, Bibb or romaine lettuce. Unless sold packaged and labeled "ready to use," mesclun should be washed and spun-dried before using.

Salad Toppers

To dress up your greens for the dinner plate, try these additions:

- thinly sliced, cold medium-rare steak
- smoked salmon or gravlax
- marinated and grilled chicken strips
- cold poached salmon pieces
- deli-purchased cold small "salad" shrimp
- deli-purchased marinated olives, artichokes, antipasto mix or roasted peppers
- bottled marinated artichokes, roasted peppers or antipasto
- store-bought Greek salad, seafood salad or shrimp mix

If you prefer a warm salad, sauté any of the following items and spoon over greens. Use just a dash of vinegar or freshly squeezed lemon juice to finish off:

- Sauté sliced mushrooms in olive oil with black pepper. Then add a dash of sherry and balsamic vinegar.

- Sauté shrimp in olive oil. Add dill and lemon zest and a squeeze of lemon juice.

- Stir-fry chicken or beef strips with sliced onions. Liberally sprinkle with chili powder, cumin and garlic powder. Add chopped tomatoes and avocados.

SOUPS ◆ Cold

CHUNKY SUPPER GAZPACHO (see recipe page 116) is the ultimate healthy refresher soup. Here it's updated with a little feta.

SOUPS ◆ Cold

ICED BORSCHT

A creamy ruby broth brimming with grated beets is a beautiful way to begin a grilled dinner.

Coarsely grate into a large bowl
   2 (14-oz/398-mL) cans drained whole beets
In a small bowl, whisk together
   10-oz (284-mL) can undiluted beef broth
   1 cup light sour cream
   1 minced garlic clove
   2 tbsp finely chopped fresh dill
   ¼ tsp each granulated sugar and freshly
      ground black pepper
Stir into beets. Cover and refrigerate until cold, at least 1 hour. Serve with a swirl of sour cream and a sprinkle of chives, sliced green onion or fresh dill.
Makes: 5½ cups

PREPARATION: 10 MINUTES
REFRIGERATION: 1 HOUR

MAKE AHEAD: Borscht will keep well, covered and refrigerated, for 2 days.

CHIC CELERIAC SOUP

This upscale combo was inspired by a soup from Tamas Ronyai, executive chef of the Ontario Club.

In a large saucepan, bring to a boil
   8 cups chicken broth or bouillon
   3 peeled cored ripe pears
   1 coarsely chopped onion
   1 peeled coarsely chopped celeriac
   1 tbsp Dijon
Reduce heat, cover and simmer until celeriac is very tender, about 30 minutes. In a blender or food processor, purée with
   ¼ tsp white or black pepper

Cover and refrigerate until cold, about 2 hours. Serve with a swirl of sour cream, finely chopped red pepper and sprigs of fresh mint. Soup is also good hot.
Makes: 12 cups for 8 to 12 servings

PREPARATION: 20 MINUTES
COOKING: 30 MINUTES
REFRIGERATION: 2 HOURS

MAKE AHEAD: Soup will keep well, covered and refrigerated, for up to 3 days or freeze.

DOUBLE MELON SOUP

Two different colored melons combine in one bowl for this terrific low-cal soup.

In a blender or food processor, purée
   ½ peeled seeded large ripe honeydew
      melon, cut into chunks
   2 tsp freshly squeezed lime juice
Pour into a 2-cup measuring cup. Then purée
   ½ peeled seeded ripe large cantaloupe,
      cut into chunks
   2 tsp freshly squeezed lime juice
Pour into another measuring cup. Cover and refrigerate separately until cold, about 1 hour. Stir or whisk into each
   2 tbsp yogurt (optional)
To serve, stir each soup. Then pour each soup simultaneously into opposite sides of a soup bowl. Draw a knife from one soup into the other to form a swirled pattern.
Makes: 4 cups

PREPARATION: 10 MINUTES
REFRIGERATION: 1 HOUR

MAKE AHEAD: Purée soups and cover and refrigerate separately for up to a day.

TWO-TONE MELON-BERRY SOUP

*Pale green and bright strawberry red complement each other beautifully
in this elegant summer soup.*

In a blender or food processor, purée
  ½ peeled seeded ripe honeydew melon,
    cut into chunks
  2 tbsp freshly squeezed lime juice
Pour into a 2-cup measuring cup. Purée
  1 pint (2 cups) hulled fresh strawberries
  2 tbsp granulated sugar
  2 tbsp apple juice or water
Pour into another measuring cup. Cover
  and refrigerate separately until cold,
  about 1 hour.

To serve, stir each soup. Then pour each soup
  simultaneously into opposite sides of a soup
  bowl. Draw a knife from one soup into the
  other to form a swirled pattern.
Serve with Curried Garlic Sticks (see recipe
  page 41).
Makes: 4 cups

PREPARATION: 10 MINUTES
REFRIGERATION: 1 HOUR

MAKE AHEAD: Purée soups and cover
and refrigerate separately, for 2 days.

TWO-TONE MELON-BERRY SOUP

COOL APPLE SOUP

This cool number is a great starter when a gorgeous rack of pork or pork tenderloin heads the menu.

In a large saucepan over medium heat, melt
   2 tbsp butter
Add
   2 finely chopped onions
   2 finely chopped celery stalks
Stir often until softened, about 5 minutes. Add
   6 chopped peeled large ripe apples,
      about 3 lbs (1.5 kg)
   ½ tsp dried leaf thyme
   ¼ tsp each ground cinnamon and nutmeg
Stir in
   7 cups chicken broth or bouillon
Bring to a boil. Reduce heat, cover and simmer, stirring occasionally, until apples are tender, about 20 minutes. In a blender or food processor, purée until almost smooth. Refrigerate until chilled, about 2 hours.
Stir in
   ½ cup half-and-half cream (optional)
Soup is also good hot.
   Makes: 6 servings

PREPARATION: 20 MINUTES
COOKING: 25 MINUTES
REFRIGERATION: 2 HOURS

MAKE AHEAD: Covered and refrigerated, soup without added cream will keep well for 2 to 3 days or freeze.

HONEYDEW-LIME SOUP

This is probably the best three-ingredient soup you'll ever make – and definitely one of the healthiest.

In a blender or food processor, purée until smooth
   1 peeled seeded ripe honeydew melon,
      cut into chunks
   juice of 1 lime
Whisk in
   ½ to 1 cup buttermilk, yogurt or
      light sour cream
Refrigerate until chilled, about 1 hour.
Serve sprinkled with shredded lime peel or chopped fresh mint.
   Makes: 6 to 8 servings

PREPARATION: 10 MINUTES
REFRIGERATION: 1 HOUR

MAKE AHEAD: Covered and refrigerated, soup will keep well for several days.

CREAM OF MANGO SOUP

This is a stunning soup that you can make a few minutes before serving.

In a blender or food processor, purée until smooth
   2 peeled ripe large mangoes
   1 to 2 cups half-and-half cream
   ½ tsp vanilla
   pinch of ground ginger
Taste and stir in if needed
   1 to 2 tbsp freshly squeezed lime juice
Refrigerate until chilled, about 1 hour or up to a day. If soups thickens, thin with milk or water.
   Makes: 6 to 8 servings

PREPARATION: 10 MINUTES

MAKE AHEAD: Covered and refrigerated, soup will keep well for several days.

CARROT & MANGO SOUP

Beta-carotene-rich carrots and mangoes top the charts of nutritious foods. They're combined here in this refreshing soup with just enough fruity taste to be really interesting.

In a large saucepan over medium, heat
　1 tbsp olive oil
Add
　1 chopped large onion
　1 ¼ tsp curry powder
Cook, stirring occasionally, until onion has softened and mixture is very fragrant, about 5 minutes.
Add
　6 to 7 chopped peeled large carrots
　4 cups chicken broth or bouillon
　½ cup orange juice
　½ tsp salt
Cover and bring to a boil. Reduce heat and simmer, stirring occasionally, until carrots are very tender, about 30 minutes.

In a food processor, purée as smooth as possible
　2 chopped peeled very large ripe mangoes
Turn into a bowl. When carrots are tender, purée in batches. Return to saucepan. Stir in mango purée. Stir often over medium-low, until hot, about 5 minutes. Refrigerate and serve cold with a scattering of snipped chives. Also great hot.
Makes: 8 cups

PREPARATION: 25 MINUTES
COOKING: 35 MINUTES

MAKE AHEAD: Covered and refrigerated, soup will keep well for up to 3 days or freeze.

CARROT & MANGO SOUP

SOUPS ◆ Hot

Ripe fragrant pears add a seductive taste in
CARROT & PEAR SOUP (see recipe page 124).

SOUPS ◆ Hot

CARROT & PEAR SOUP

*Ripe pears or apples give body and a very
intriguing taste to this easy and healthy soup.*

In a large saucepan, melt
    1 tbsp butter
Add
    1 chopped large onion
    1 minced garlic clove
Cook until onion has softened, about 5 minutes.
    Add
    4 cups chicken broth or bouillon
    4 large chopped carrots
        or 2 chopped peeled sweet potatoes
    4 chopped peeled pears or apples
    ½ tsp salt
    ¼ tsp cayenne or white pepper
Cover and bring to a boil. Reduce heat and
    simmer until carrots are very tender,
    about 30 minutes. Purée in a blender
    or food processor. Reheat until hot.
Taste and if needed add
    1 tsp granulated sugar
Serve with a scattering of snipped chives.
    Makes: 5 to 8 cups for 5 to 8 servings

*PREPARATION: 25 MINUTES
COOKING: 35 MINUTES*

MAKE AHEAD: After puréeing soup,
cover and refrigerate for up to
2 days or freeze.

EASY ELEGANT SOUP

*Asparagus, slivers of mushroom and red pepper in a
soothing broth add up to a sophisticated spring starter.*

In a large saucepan, combine
    2 (10-oz) cans chicken broth, preferably
        lower sodium
    ¼ cup sherry
    1 tbsp freshly squeezed lemon juice
    4 thin slices fresh ginger
    ¼ tsp salt
Bring to a boil over medium heat. When boiling,
    stir in
    ¼ lb (125 g) sliced mixed mushrooms,
        such as shiitake, oyster and button
    2 cups diagonally sliced asparagus
    1 chopped seeded small red pepper
    2 thinly sliced green onions
    1 cup diced cooked chicken (optional)
Heat until asparagus is just cooked, about
    5 minutes. Remove ginger and serve.
    Makes: 7 cups

*PREPARATION: 10 MINUTES
COOKING: 8 MINUTES*

MAKE AHEAD: Prepare soup base. Add
mushrooms, peppers and chicken and
refrigerate immediately for up to a day.
Add asparagus and onions and reheat.

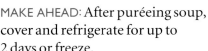

Easy Elegant Soup

ORIENTAL THREE-MUSHROOM SOUP

*Extremely elegant and light sum up
this stunning soup starter.*

In a large saucepan over high heat, combine
    4 cups water
    10 whole dried shiitake or black mushrooms
    1/4 cup mirin or rice wine
    2 tbsp fish sauce or 2 tbsp teriyaki sauce
Bring to a boil, then remove from heat and let
    stand, 15 minutes. Remove mushrooms
    from broth. Remove and discard stems.
    Slice mushrooms and return to broth.
    Place pan over medium-high heat. Stir in
    1/4 lb (125 g) sliced button mushrooms
When boiling, stir in
    1/4 lb (125 g) enoki mushrooms
    2 thinly sliced green onions
Heat and serve.
    Makes: 4 cups for 4 servings

PREPARATION: 15 MINUTES
COOKING: 10 MINUTES

MAKE AHEAD: Prepare soup without
enoki mushrooms and green onions.
Cover and refrigerate for up to 2 days.
Reheat until hot, then add enoki
mushrooms and green onions.

MULTI-BEAN SOUP

*Here's a great warm starter to serve in mugs around
the fireplace after a day of skiing or snowmobiling.*

In a large saucepan over medium-high heat,
    combine
    1 cup chicken broth or bouillon
    2 chopped onions
    2 chopped carrots
    2 chopped celery stalks
    1/4 cup barley
    1 minced garlic clove
Bring to a boil. Stir in
    7 cups chicken broth or bouillon
    28-oz can diced tomatoes, including juice
    1 chopped seeded red or green pepper
    1 bay leaf
    1/4 tsp each dried leaf thyme, freshly ground
        black pepper and cayenne
Bring to a boil, cover and simmer, 20 minutes.
    Stir in
    3 (19-oz) cans rinsed drained beans,
        preferably a mix of red, white and black
Taste and add a squeeze of lemon juice
    if needed.
When hot, stir in
    1/2 cup chopped fresh parsley (optional)
    Makes: 14 cups for 7 servings

PREPARATION: 20 MINUTES
COOKING: 30 MINUTES

MAKE AHEAD: Covered and refrigerated,
soup will keep well for 3 days or freeze.

SOUPS ◆ Hot

CHUNKY TOMATO SOUP

This light soup takes 10 minutes to make. Serve with Multi-Cheese Croutons (see recipe page 46).

In a medium-size saucepan, melt
   1 tbsp butter
Add
   2 finely chopped shallots
      or 1 minced garlic clove
   1 chopped celery stalk
   1 chopped carrot
   1 tsp each dried basil and granulated sugar
Sauté, stirring frequently, until vegetables have
   softened, about 5 minutes. Add
   28-oz can diced tomatoes, including juice
Boil gently, uncovered and stirring often,
   to blend flavors and thicken, from 3 to
   5 minutes.
   Makes: 4 servings

PREPARATION: 10 MINUTES
COOKING: 10 MINUTES

MAKE AHEAD: Covered and refrigerated, soup keeps well for 2 days.

MEXICAN TOMATO SOUP

A fresh tomato soup, tarted up with hot peppers, is a great way to start a barbecued dinner.

In a large saucepan, heat
   1 tbsp vegetable or olive oil
Add
   4 finely chopped onions
   2 chopped seeded hot peppers
   3 minced garlic cloves
Cook, stirring occasionally, until softened, about
   10 minutes. Stir in
   1 tsp ground cumin
   ½ tsp freshly ground black pepper
Add
   10 chopped seeded peeled tomatoes
   5 cups vegetable juice

Bring to a boil. Reduce heat and simmer,
   uncovered, for 15 minutes. Taste and
   add pinches of salt and granulated sugar
   if needed.
Serve sprinkled with chopped fresh coriander.
   Makes: 8 cups

PREPARATION: 30 MINUTES
COOKING: 25 MINUTES

MAKE AHEAD: Covered and refrigerated, soup keeps well for up to 2 days or freeze.

LOW-FAT CURRIED LENTIL SOUP

The protein content of lentils makes this a healthy beginning for a comfort dinner.

In a large saucepan, melt
   1 tbsp butter
Add
   2 chopped large onions
   4 minced garlic cloves
   1 to 2 tsp curry powder
Cook until onion has softened, about 5 minutes.
   Stir in
   6 cups chicken broth or bouillon
   4 sliced carrots
   3 sliced celery stalks
   1 chopped seeded green pepper
   1¼ cups rinsed red lentils
   1 tbsp ground cumin
   ½ to 1 tsp hot red pepper flakes
Bring to a boil and skim off any foam that forms.
   Cover, reduce heat to low and simmer until
   lentils are tender, about 20 minutes.
   Makes: 10 cups for 10 servings

PREPARATION: 10 MINUTES
COOKING: 25 MINUTES

MAKE AHEAD: Covered and refrigerated, soup keeps well for several days or freeze.

Leek & Potato Shrimp Chowder

Set a special mood for a winter dinner with this upscale chowder.
Use shrimp or tiny bay scallops or a combination of the two.

In a large saucepan, cook until crisp, about
   5 minutes
   2 strips bacon, cut into narrow strips
Remove and set aside.
Stir into fat in pan
   4 medium leeks, cleaned and thinly sliced
   1 minced garlic clove
Sauté over medium heat until leeks have
   softened, about 8 minutes. Add
   2 finely diced peeled large potatoes
   4 cups chicken broth or bouillon
Bring to a boil, then reduce heat, cover and
   simmer, stirring occasionally, until potatoes
   are tender, from 15 to 20 minutes. Stir in
   $\frac{1}{2}$ lb (250 g) peeled small shrimp or scallops

Cook until hot and almost firm, from
   3 to 5 minutes. Stir in
   1 cup homogenized milk or table cream
   2 tbsp chopped fresh parsley
   or dill (optional)
   $\frac{1}{4}$ tsp freshly ground black pepper
Heat, but do not boil. Taste and add salt if needed.
Makes: 8 cups for about 8 servings

PREPARATION: 10 MINUTES
COOKING: 38 MINUTES

MAKE AHEAD: Covered and
refrigerated, soup keeps well
for up to 2 days.

LEEK & POTATO SHRIMP CHOWDER

SOUPS ◆ Hot

Jalapeño Santa Fe Chowder

*This hearty tomato chowder brims
with Southwestern flavors.*

In a large saucepan, heat
    I tbsp olive or vegetable oil
Stir in
    I chopped onion
    4 minced garlic cloves
Cook until onion has softened, about 5 minutes.
    Stir in
    I tbsp ground cumin
    I tsp chili powder
    ½ tsp dried leaf oregano
Cook for 2 minutes. Add
    28-oz can diced tomatoes, including juice
    2 cups chicken broth or bouillon
    I chopped green pepper
    2 chopped celery stalks
    I to 3 finely chopped seeded
       jalapeño peppers
Bring to a boil. Then cover, reduce heat and
    simmer, 10 minutes. Stir in
    I cup kernel corn
Cook for 5 minutes. Serve sprinkled with grated
    cheddar and lightly crushed corn chips.
Makes: 7 cups for 6 to 8 servings

PREPARATION: 20 MINUTES
COOKING: 22 MINUTES

MAKE AHEAD: Covered and
refrigerated, soup will keep well
for up to 2 days. Or freeze for up
to 2 months.

Confetti Corn Chowder

*Turn the heat up on popular corn chowder with hot
red pepper flakes and hot pickled peppers.*

In a large saucepan over medium heat, melt
    2 tbsp butter
Add
    I chopped onion
    I chopped green pepper
Sauté until softened, about 5 minutes. Then,
    while stirring, sprinkle with
    ⅓ cup all-purpose flour
Stir until absorbed. Slowly stir in
    2 cups chicken broth or bouillon
    2 tsp Dijon
    ½ tsp each paprika, hot red pepper flakes
       and salt
Cook, stirring frequently, until thickened, from
    5 to 8 minutes. Stir in
    2 cups kernel corn
    2 to 3 finely cubed peeled potatoes
Stir frequently and bring to a boil. Then reduce
    heat, cover and simmer, stirring occasionally,
    until potatoes are tender, about 20 minutes.
    Stir in
    3 cups milk
    ¼ cup well-drained chopped pickled peppers
       (optional)
Serve sprinkled with thinly sliced green onions.
Makes: 8 cups, 8 servings

PREPARATION: 15 MINUTES
COOKING: 33 MINUTES

MAKE AHEAD: Covered and
refrigerated, soup will keep well
for 2 days.

SHRIMP & VEGETABLE SOUP

This stunning seafood-flavored soup is almost fat-free and a light and elegant beginning to dinner.

In a small dish, soak
  2 (0.3-oz/10-g) pkgs sliced dried mushrooms
  in
  1 cup hot water
Meanwhile, in a large saucepan, combine
  10-oz can undiluted chicken broth,
    preferably lower sodium
  3¾ cups water
Bring to a boil over medium-high heat. Rinse,
  then add to broth
  1 lb (500 g) fresh or frozen uncooked
    medium shrimp with shells
As soon as broth returns to a boil, remove from
  heat. Immediately remove all the shrimp.
  Shell shrimp, returning shells to broth.
  Refrigerate shelled shrimp. Add to broth

  2-inch (5-cm) knob thinly sliced fresh ginger
  ¼ tsp hot red pepper flakes
Bring to a boil. Reduce heat, cover and simmer,
  15 minutes. Strain broth and discard solids.
  Return to pan and bring to a boil. Stir in
  soaked mushrooms, soaking liquid, shelled
  shrimp and
  8 large julienned snow peas or spinach leaves
  1 small chopped red pepper
  2 tbsp sherry or brandy (optional)
Cook for 1 minute or just until shrimp are hot.
  Serve immediately.
Makes: 6 cups for 6 servings

PREPARATION: 20 MINUTES
COOKING: 25 MINUTES

SHRIMP & VEGETABLE SOUP

MUSSEL & JALAPEÑO CHOWDER

*Serve this hearty chowder, spiked with jalapeños,
with Curried Garlic Sticks (see recipe page 41).*

In a large saucepan, heat
    2 tsp vegetable oil
Add
    1 large chopped onion
    2 chopped seeded jalapeños
      or 2 tbsp canned chopped green chilies
    2 minced garlic cloves
Cook, stirring occasionally until onion has
    softened, about 5 minutes. Stir in
    28-oz can diced tomatoes, including juice
    ½ cup white wine
    1 tsp each dried tarragon and dillweed
    ¼ tsp cayenne
Bring to a boil, reduce heat and simmer,
    covered, for 5 minutes. Add
    2 lbs (1 kg) scrubbed mussels
    ½ lb (250 g) mild-flavored fish fillets,
      cut into bite-size pieces
Cover and simmer until mussels open, from
    8 to 10 minutes. Discard any mussels that
    do not open.
Makes: 4 to 6 servings

PREPARATION: 10 MINUTES
COOKING: 20 MINUTES

MAKE AHEAD: Prepare chowder base
but don't add seafood. Refrigerate
for up to 2 days or freeze. Reheat,
then add seafood.

THAI CHOWDER

*This addictive soup will wake up the taste buds
at the beginning of any dinner party.*

In a large bowl, cover with boiling water
    4 oz (120 g) broad Oriental rice
      stick noodles
Soak while making broth, at least 15 minutes,
    then drain. Meanwhile, in a large saucepan
    over high heat, bring to a boil
    6 cups chicken broth or bouillon
    1-inch (2.5-cm) piece fresh ginger, sliced
    2 slightly crushed garlic cloves
    2 whole dried hot red peppers
      or ½ tsp hot red pepper flakes
    6 chopped green onions, white portion only
      (reserve green parts for later)
    1 thickly sliced lemongrass stalk
    2 tbsp fish sauce
Reduce heat and simmer, covered, 20 minutes.
    Reserving broth, strain out solids and
    discard. Heat strained broth until boiling,
    about 2 minutes. Stir in drained noodles and
    2 cups sliced shiitake, oyster or button
      mushrooms
    1 lb (500 g) raw or cooked fresh or frozen,
      peeled large shrimp
    2 tbsp freshly squeezed lime or lemon juice
    1 to 3 tsp hot Oriental chili-garlic sauce
    ¼ cup chopped fresh coriander
Simmer gently, stirring occasionally, until
    soup is hot and shrimp are pink, from 3 to
    5 minutes. Serve right away sprinkled with
    thinly sliced green portion of green onions.
Makes: 9 cups for about 8 servings

PREPARATION: 20 MINUTES
COOKING: 30 MINUTES

CLASSIC OYSTER SOUP

*Start Christmas dinner or any special party
with this simple, yet sublime, soup.*

In a large saucepan over medium-low heat,
combine
2 cups homogenized milk
1 cup half-and-half cream
2 tbsp butter
2 tbsp vermouth
1 bay leaf
¼ tsp hot pepper sauce
pinch of ground nutmeg
Cover and heat until hot, but not yet simmering,
about 5 minutes. Stir in
3 cups shucked oysters, including juice,
or 3 (5-oz) cans whole oysters
Cover and heat until oyster edges just start
to curl or canned oysters are heated through,
about 3 minutes. Remove bay leaf and serve
sprinkled with chopped fresh parsley.
Makes: 6 cups

*PREPARATION: 15 MINUTES
COOKING: 8 MINUTES*

MAKE AHEAD: Prepare soup base,
without oysters, and refrigerate for
up to 2 days. Reheat, then add oysters
and continue with recipe.

LOUISIANA SOUP

*Here's a laid-back way to a thick spicy
fish-and-rice soup starter.*

In a large saucepan, heat
10-oz can undiluted chicken broth
1 cup water
2 tbsp salsa
2 thinly sliced celery stalks
1 chopped green pepper
When hot, stir in
½ cup quick-cooking rice
6.5-oz (184-g) can drained tuna
¼ tsp each dried leaf thyme and paprika
Heat until piping hot and serve.
Makes: 4 cups for 2 to 3 servings

*PREPARATION: 10 MINUTES
COOKING: 15 MINUTES*

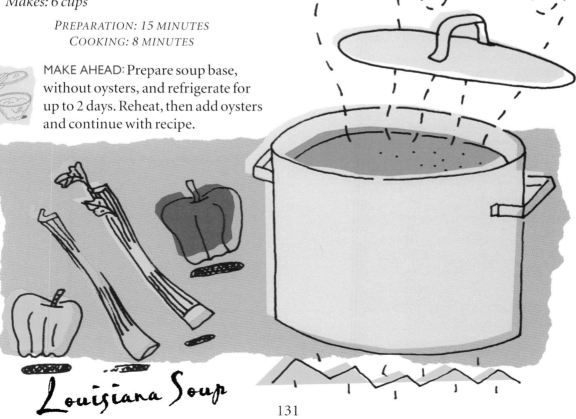

Louisiana Soup

SOUPS ◆ Hot

131

CHICKEN-CREOLE SOUP

Bacon gives a smoky taste to this hearty soup, but there's still lots of flavor if you make it without.

In a large saucepan over medium heat, cook
until crisp, about 5 minutes
  6 strips bacon, cut into narrow strips
Drain bacon on paper towel and discard all but
a tablespoon of fat, or heat
  1 tbsp vegetable oil
Add
  2 coarsely chopped large onions
  4 minced garlic cloves
Sauté until onions have softened, about
5 minutes. Stir in bacon pieces and
  4 cups chicken broth or bouillon
  28-oz can diced tomatoes, including juice
  2 bay leaves
  1 tsp each chili powder, dried leaf thyme,
    hot pepper sauce and Worcestershire
Submerge in liquid
  4 to 6 skinless, bone-in chicken breasts
    or legs
Bring to a boil, skimming off any foam which
forms. Simmer 20 minutes, then stir in
  ½ cup uncooked rice
  2 chopped large green peppers
  2 chopped celery stalks
  ½ tsp coarsely ground black pepper
Cover soup and simmer another 20 minutes.
Remove chicken and separate from the
bones and slice. Stir into soup and heat
until piping hot.
Makes: 12 cups for 8 to 10 servings

PREPARATION: 30 MINUTES
COOKING: 50 MINUTES

MAKE AHEAD: Covered and
refrigerated, soup will keep well
for 3 days or freeze.

ORIENTAL CHICKEN NOODLE SOUP

Make this wonderful soup with either thick slices of bok choy, or shrimp and snow peas.

Rinse under warm water
  10 dried mushrooms
Soak in
  1 cup hot water
Meanwhile, in a large saucepan, combine
  6 cups chicken broth or bouillon
  2 cups water
  2 tbsp sherry
  1 tbsp soy sauce
  1 tsp dark sesame oil
  ½ to 1 tsp hot red pepper flakes
  2 minced garlic cloves
  1-inch (2.5-cm) knob fresh ginger, thinly sliced
Bring to a boil. Add
  2 skinless, boneless chicken breasts,
    cut into strips
Reduce heat, cover and simmer until chicken is
cooked, from 6 to 8 minutes. Meanwhile,
place in a sieve and rinse with warm water
  ½ (1-lb/450-g) pkg rice stick noodles, about
    ¼ inch (0.5 cm) wide
Then set aside. Remove stems from the
soaking mushrooms and discard. Thinly
slice. Stir mushrooms and soaking liquid
into broth with noodles and
  4 thinly sliced green onions
Heat until noodles are "al dente." Serve right away.
Makes: 8 cups

PREPARATION: 15 MINUTES
COOKING: 15 MINUTES

MAKE AHEAD: Prepare broth,
simmering chicken until cooked.
Discard mushroom stems, slice
mushrooms and add along with
cooking liquid. Cover and refrigerate for
up to 2 days. Reheat. Stir in rinsed noodles
and green onions.

CHICKEN & SHIITAKE SOUP WITH COCONUT MILK

Coconut milk gives a sublime flavor to this elegant soup,
yet it takes mere minutes to make.

In a large saucepan, combine
    2 cups chicken broth or bouillon
    14-oz (400-mL) can light or regular
      unsweetened coconut milk
    ¼ cup finely chopped fresh ginger
    ½ tsp hot red pepper flakes or 1 small hot
      chopped seeded red pepper
    1 tbsp fish sauce
    grated peel of 1 lime
    1 tbsp freshly squeezed lime juice
Cover and bring to a boil. Stir in
    2 skinless, boneless chicken breasts,
      cut into strips
    2 to 3 sliced shiitake mushrooms

Reduce heat, cover and simmer until chicken is
    cooked, from 6 to 8 minutes. Stir in
    ¼ cup chopped fresh coriander
    2 thinly sliced green onions
Stir in more lime juice if needed.
    Makes: 5½ cups for 6 servings

      PREPARATION: 10 MINUTES
      COOKING: 12 MINUTES

 MAKE AHEAD: Covered and
refrigerated, soup will keep well
for 1 day.

CHICKEN & SHIITAKE SOUP WITH COCONUT MILK

CHICKEN-COCONUT SOUP

With lemongrass, coriander and ginger, this satiny soup delivers the best flavors of the Orient.

In a large saucepan over medium heat, combine
  2 cups chicken broth or bouillon
  14-oz (400-mL) can light or regular
    unsweetened coconut milk
  ¼ cup grated fresh ginger
  3 lemongrass stalks, split lengthwise
  ½ to 1 small finely chopped seeded
    hot pepper
  1 tbsp fish sauce
  finely grated peel of 1 lime
  1 tbsp freshly squeezed lime juice
Bring to a boil and stir in
  2 skinless, boneless chicken breasts,
    cut into strips
Reduce heat, cover and simmer until chicken
  is cooked, from 6 to 8 minutes. Remove and
  discard lemongrass. Stir in
  ¼ cup coarsely chopped fresh coriander
  2 thinly sliced green onions
Taste and add more lime juice if needed.
  Makes: 6 cups for 6 servings

  PREPARATION: 10 MINUTES
  COOKING: 8 MINUTES

MAKE AHEAD: Covered and refrigerated, soup will keep well for 1 day. Do not freeze.

SWEET POTATO SOUP

This yummy soup gets a double dose of beta-carotene-rich vegetables with carrots and sweet potatoes.

Trim root and dark green ends from
  1 large leek
Cut in half lengthwise and rinse under cold
  running water. Slice leek and
  2 peeled carrots
  into ½-inch (1-cm) pieces.
In a large saucepan over medium-low, melt
  1 to 2 tbsp butter
Add leek. Cook, stirring often, until softened
  slightly, about 2 minutes. Add carrots and
  4 cups chicken broth or bouillon
Increase heat to medium-high. Meanwhile,
  peel and cut into quarters
  3 sweet potatoes
Add to broth. Cover and bring to a boil.
  Reduce heat and simmer, covered, for at least
  20 minutes, until vegetables are soft. Remove
  from heat. Drain broth into a bowl. In a food
  processor, purée vegetables in 2 or 3 batches,
  adding ½ cup broth to each batch. Stir in
  remaining broth and
  ⅛ tsp each salt and white pepper
Pour into bowls and top each serving with
  1 tsp sour cream
  Makes: 6 cups

  PREPARATION: 20 MINUTES
  COOKING: 25 MINUTES

MAKE AHEAD: Covered and refrigerated, soup will keep well for several days and freezes well.

GRAND STARTER SOUP WITH CHICKEN & SPINACH

This proves a great chicken soup doesn't have to begin with a whole bird.
Cans of broth and boneless breasts speed up the process.

In a large saucepan, heat
    1 tbsp olive oil
Add
    2 minced garlic cloves
    1 tbsp minced fresh ginger
Sauté 2 minutes. Add
    2 skinless, boneless chicken breasts,
      cut into strips
Cook and stir often until pink color is gone. Add
    2 (10-oz) cans undiluted chicken broth,
      preferably lower sodium
    1 soup can water
    3 thinly sliced carrots
Bring to a boil, cover and reduce heat. Simmer
    until carrots are tender, about 20 minutes.

Just before serving, stir in
    3½ cups torn spinach leaves
    ¼ tsp freshly ground black pepper
    2 (19-oz) cans drained rinsed mixed beans
      (optional)
Heat until hot and serve with crusty bread.
    Makes: 6 cups for 6 servings

PREPARATION: 15 MINUTES
COOKING: 30 MINUTES

MAKE AHEAD: Prepare soup without spinach and black pepper. Cover and refrigerate for up to 2 days. Reheat, then add spinach and black pepper.

GRAND STARTER SOUP WITH CHICKEN & SPINACH

FENNEL & SQUASH SOUP

Fennel's mild anise flavor jazzes up squash, so this soup tastes rich
without any added cream.

Cut green fronds from
    1 bulb fennel
Save to garnish soup. Remove core from bulb.
    Thickly slice bulb and white parts of fronds.
    In a large saucepan over medium heat, melt
    1 tbsp butter
Add
    1 chopped onion
    1 chopped large celery stalk
Cook until onion has softened, about 5 minutes.
    Stir in fennel and
    1 peeled seeded squash, cut into cubes
Pour in enough to cover vegetables from
    2 (10-oz) cans chicken broth and 2 cups
    water or 4½ cups chicken or vegetable
    bouillon

Bring to a boil. Reduce heat, cover and simmer until vegetables are very tender, from 15 to 30 minutes. In a food processor, purée in several batches. Return to saucepan. Stir in remaining water or bouillon. Heat, stirring often, until hot, but not boiling. Taste and add salt if needed. Ladle soup into soup bowls, then float a small piece of saved green fennel on top.
Makes: 6 cups

PREPARATION: 20 MINUTES
COOKING: 30 MINUTES

MAKE AHEAD: Covered and refrigerated, soup will keep well for up to 3 days or frozen for up to a month.

Fennel & Squash Soup

TIPS

Soup Sense

- Stock is the base for many soups. The better the stock, the better the soup. If you don't have a homemade stock, there are excellent canned varieties available. Just remember that unless the recipe calls for the actual can of undiluted chicken stock, you should dilute the stock following directions on the side of the can.

- Most soups can be frozen. If they involve vegetables, add a few slices of fresh vegetables for a crisp texture when you reheat.

- To give some extra oomph to your soups, stir in some chopped fresh garlic, chopped chives, coriander or parsley, or even grated orange or lemon peel just before serving.

- Most soups benefit from sitting in the refrigerator overnight.

- Another way to add texture to vegetable soups is to hold back about a quarter of the sliced or chopped veggies called for in a recipe and add them for the last 5 to 10 minutes of cooking.

- For an elegant finishing touch, stir in a tablespoon or two of wine or liqueur just before serving. Try brandy in a French onion soup, sherry in an Oriental broth or cream soup, red wine for hearty soups and white wine for chicken or seafood chowders.

- Don't add sour cream until the last few minutes of cooking or it may curdle.

- Consider croutons made from pumpernickel, rye or whole-grain breads or float a small slice of garlic bread in the centre of the soup.

Taste Test

- Always remember to taste the soup before adding any additional salt. If a recipe calls for a can of sodium-reduced chicken broth and you use regular chicken broth, don't add any additional salt until you've finished the soup and tasted it.

- Add ground pepper just before serving. It can become bitter if simmered in a soup too long.

- A pinch of sugar will always improve a tomato-based soup.

- If your soup is too salty, float a few slices of potato on top of the soup and simmer. Then discard.

INDEX

INDEX

CREDITS

ILLUSTRATIONS by Jeff Jackson
PHOTOGRAPHS
Michael Mahovlich: pages 71, 79, 101, 127, 129
Claude Noel: page 27
Ed O'Neil: front cover and pages 9, 13, 17, 19, 31, 33, 37, 43, 49, 53, 57, 63, 65, 67, 73, 75, 83, 85, 89, 91, 95, 97, 105, 107, 111, 115, 119, 121, 123, 135
Christopher Reardon: page 21

CHATELAINE food express
Starters

FOR SMITH SHERMAN BOOKS INC.

EDITORIAL DIRECTOR
Carol Sherman

ART DIRECTOR
Andrew Smith

SENIOR EDITOR
Bernice Eisenstein

ASSOCIATE EDITOR
Erik Tanner

PAGE LAYOUT AND COMPOSITION
Joseph Gisini

COLOR SEPARATIONS
T-C4 Graphics Ltd., Winnipeg

PRINTING
Kromar Printing Ltd., Winnipeg

SMITH SHERMAN BOOKS INC.
533 College Street, Suite 402,
Toronto, Canada M6G 1A8
e-mail: bloke@total.net

FOR CHATELAINE

FOOD EDITOR
Monda Rosenberg

TEST KITCHEN ASSISTANT
Trudy Patterson

SENIOR COPY EDITOR
Deborah Aldcorn

CHATELAINE ADVISORY BOARD
Rona Maynard, Lee Simpson

PROJECT MANAGER
Cheryl Smith

CHATELAINE, MACLEAN HUNTER
PUBLISHING LIMITED
777 Bay Street,
Toronto, Canada M5W 1A7
e-mail: letters@chatelaine.com

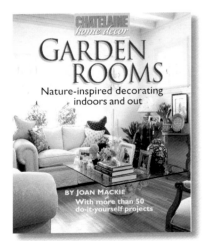
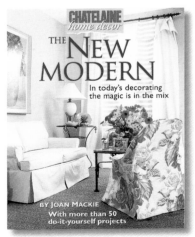
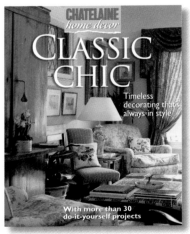